"Jasmin speaks to the hea[rt of the addict. He]r writing [tau]ght me to walk through my fear. It saved my life. At fifty-one she taught me how to be happy."
—JULIA GINDI

"I did not understand the disease. Although I've read dozens of self-help books for twenty years, I had no clue until I read Jasmin's work. Without it I would not have been able to stay sober—and I do mean that. It helped me to stop hating and resenting myself, and to see that this is part of the disease. I had never understood why I had behaved like that, and that is why I could not stop beating myself up in sobriety. Every recovering addict can benefit from reading this book."
—R.P.

"This book helped me to understand the feelings I was going through sober and why. It helped me to accept it and be O.K. with the process."
—INGRID DELALIAN

"Jasmin's writing gives me hope and peace of mind that I am not alone in recovery. She is brilliant with metaphors and speaking to her readers in a relatable way. Her writings were instrumental and at many times lifesaving in my early recovery. Her writing makes me feel safe, encouraged, and optimistic."
—KELLIE LINDBACK

"Jasmin's writing is phenomenal and extraordinary. It helped me to believe in myself."
—BLAKE NEWSTED

"Breathtaking. Fabulous! Only Jasmin can make this so tangible for me. I'm enthusiastic!"
—ARIANE THIEDE

"Jasmin saved my life. Her writing inspires me and gives me strength."
—LEON HENDRIX, BROTHER OF JIMI HENDRIX

"Jasmin's writings are integral to my serenity. She explains profound ideas in a tangible and palatable manner, imparting an immediate feeling of hope. Her book makes recovery accessible and provides me with a deep sense of comfort and peace, a sense that everything will be O.K. and that I am not alone. It is the perfect daily reader for me."
—Delfina Hasiwar

"The way I see it, Jasmin stayed sober strictly because she was so willing to embrace the spiritual tools. In her book she describes all that she has learned about recovery. Her book will help others stay sober as well."
—Nico Wright

"A friendly and practical guide to recovery. Uniquely, Jasmin combines personal experience as a former addict with the insight of a psychotherapist. Through easy to relate to analogies this book integrates cognitive behavioral techniques to form an awareness of thoughts and emotions, whilst giving practical advice on how to change behaviors. With concise chapters, the reader can easily seek out guidance for their problems, helping to resolve feelings of anxiety and providing accompaniment down the road to recovery."
—Isla Kriss

"A great guide for dealing with overwhelming emotions in early recovery. I loved it."
—Richard Rogg, Founder,
Promises Residential Treatment Centers

"Jasmin has put her heart, soul, wisdom and experience into the pages of this book—offering great tools for recovery."
—Donna Miller, Director,
Chabad Residential Treatment Center

TO HELL & BACK

TO HELL & BACK

HOW TO HAVE FEELINGS
& STAY SOBER AT THE SAME TIME

JASMIN ROGG, M.A., M.F.T.

VOICE OF RECOVERY PRESS
LOS ANGELES, CALIFORNIA

This publication is designed to educate and provide general information regarding the subject matter covered. It is not intended to replace the counsel of other professional advisors. The reader is encouraged to consult with his or her own advisors regarding specific situations. The author and publisher specifically disclaim any liability resulting from the use or application of the information contained in this book.

For information, contact the publisher:
Voice of Recovery Press
P.O. Box 292257, Los Angeles, CA 90029
info@voiceofrecoverypress.com
www.voiceofrecoverypress.com

Printed in the United States of America on acid-free paper.

Publisher's Cataloging-In-Publication Data

Rogg, Jasmin.
  To hell & back : how to have feelings & stay sober at the same time / Jasmin Rogg.

    p. ; cm.
    ISBN: 978-0-615-33083-9

  1. Alcoholics--Rehabilitation. 2. Drug addicts--Rehabilitation. 3. Alcoholism--Psychological aspects. 4. Drug abuse--Psychological aspects. 5. Self-help techniques. I. Title. II. Title: To hell and back

  HV5276 .R64 2010
  362.2918   2009939779

Book Producer: Brookes Nohlgren | www.BooksByBrookes.com
Cover Designer: The Book Designers | www.TheBookDesigners.com
Book Designer: Dotti Albertine | www.AlbertineBookDesign.com

*Make your recovery
your number one priority and
everything else will follow...*
—Author Unknown

BOOMERANG

THE ENERGY YOU EMIT RETURNS IN LIKE CHARGE.

WHAT YOU SEND OUT COMES BACK TO YOU LIKE A BOOMERANG.

IF YOU PUT OUT AGGRESSION, THE OTHERS WILL RESENT YOU, TOO.

IF YOU LIVE NEEDINESS AND DESIRE, YOU CREATE LACK ALL AROUND YOU.

IF YOU LIKE TO COMPLAIN, THE UNIVERSE WILL PROVIDE THINGS TO COMPLAIN ABOUT.

IF YOU DECIDE TO BRING LOVE AND JOY, THOUGH, YOU LIVE IN AN ENCHANTED WORLD,

SURROUNDED BY PEOPLE WHO ARE GLAD THAT YOU ARE HERE.

AND IF YOU BEGIN AND END EACH DAY IN GRATITUDE,

YOU ARE BLESSED WITH A GOOD LIFE.

CHECK IT OUT.

CONTENTS

Acknowledgments   *xiii*

Preface   *xv*

PART ONE | **MY STORY**   **1**

PART TWO | **ALCOHOLISM & ADDICTION**   **11**

     CATCH-22   12

     ALCOHOLIC/ADDICT   13

     ARE YOU A LITTLE GREEN FROG?   19

     SEEKING TO TAKE THE EDGE OFF   21

     HEDONISM   24

     INSANE IN THE MIDBRAIN   27

     SELF-SOOTHING   30

     AVALANCHE   32

PART THREE | **TOOLS FOR YOUR RECOVERY**   **33**

     BE YOUR OWN GOOD MOTHER   35

     DAILY MENTAL HYGIENE   38

     BREATHE AND MEDITATE   40

     BREATHING EXERCISES   42

CONTENTS

PRAYER MAGIC   44

MY TWO FAVORITE PRAYERS   46

BE STILL   47

A MEDITATION ON LETTING GO   49

VISUAL IMAGERY   51

POSITIVE AFFIRMATIONS   54

IT IS WHAT IT IS   57

A LIFE LIVED IN FEAR ISN'T MUCH FUN   58

UNTAMED MIND   62

WATER, B, C   64

PART FOUR | **RELATIONSHIPS**   **67**

RAFT PEOPLE   69

LOVING A PORCUPINE   74

A CO-DEPENDENT RELATIONSHIP   76

DRAMA   77

LOVE AN ALCOHOLIC   79

SEX & LOBSTER   80

THE PERFECT MAN   82

S&M   85

BIRDS OF A FEATHER   88

FIGHTING WITH MONSTERS   90

FAMILY FUN   92

ASSERTIVENESS   95

PART FIVE | **THIRTEEN ALCOHOLICS**   **97**

1. LARRY BREWS   99

2. RACHEL SEEKS ABUSE   101

3. LUCAN BREAKS SOME BONES   103

Contents

4. Liz in a Bottle 106
5. Gary, the Failed Big Shot 108
6. Shame Shame Shame 111
7. ...the More I Love My Cats 114
8. Flower Child 117
9. The Naïve Bouncer 120
10. Kirsten, Escape Artist 123
11. Victims R Us 126
12. Glamour Rape 129
13. Live Combat 132

PART SIX | **UNDERSTANDING RECOVERY** 135

You, Me, My Cats, and Stephen Hawking 137
The Promises 140
Psychotherapy 142
Food for Thought 143
Perception 145
Wounds 148
Red-Light District 150
Psychic Change 152
Momentum 155
Urgent Impulses 157
Radio Days 160
Anger & Aggression 164
Resentments 167
Forgiveness 172
The Most Important Thing 173
Self-Love 176

SENSE OF SELF   178
NOT YOUR RECIPES FOR MY HAPPINESS   180
RHYTHM   182
A PACT WITH THE DEVIL   184
TWO WOLVES ARE FIGHTING IN MY HEART   187
DEMONS & DESIRES   190
THE GOLDEN KEY   191
THE MAGIC OF THE SPOKEN WORD   193
THE GARDEN OF LIFE   195
WILLINGNESS   198
INITIATION   200
TIME IS ON MY SIDE   202
RELAPSE   205
MIRAGE   207

FINAL THOUGHTS   **209**
STILL STANDING   210
TWELVE-STEP PROGRAMS   211
SPIRITUAL BOOKS TO SUPPORT YOUR RECOVERY   213

Credits   *215*
About the Author   *217*

ACKNOWLEDGMENTS

THIS BOOK IS DEDICATED to my ex-husband, Richard Rogg, the founder of Promises Treatment Centers; his beautiful wife, Lisa; and their children, Myles and Sophia. I don't even want to imagine what would have become of me had he not been in my life for thirty years—like an angel. Without him, I would not have the two most precious things in my life—our beautiful son, Jesse, and my sobriety. I am more grateful than words can express for the wonderful and life-changing opportunity to get clean and sober at Promises.

A very special thank you goes to my sponsor, Nico Wright, and her husband, Larry. Nico is like a mother and sister to me. She always treated me with kindness and patience when I needed it in order to stay clean and sober. She guided me with never-ending compassion and humor. She showed me the way to a life with serenity, peace, faith, self-respect, and dignity—a good life with purpose and joy.

I am particularly grateful to the thirteen recovering alcoholics I interviewed, as well as Leon Hendrix and Delfina Hasiwar for their help, patience, and encouragement with reading and re-reading my manuscript. Thank you Marcello Altieri for the logo design, Dotti Albertine for the book design, and my book producer Brookes Nohlgren and cover designer Alan Hebel for their phenomenal talent, attitude, and dedication. What a joy it was to work with you! And a special thanks to Donna Miller, M.F.T., Dr. David Sack, and Dr. Dave Murphy.

I want to thank every single person for being in my life, but especially my family, Hellmuth Herbst, Markus Weingartner, Baerbel Stoeger, Erika Mueller, Jorid Nygard, my friends, clients, and sponsees for teaching me about love and the meaning of life.

We cannot do this life alone, and we feel worthwhile only when we relate lovingly to each other.

PREFACE

BECAUSE OF MY OWN EXPERIENCE with addiction and my gratitude for my own recovery, I have devoted my life to helping
other recovering alcoholics/addicts. Since my Marriage Family
Therapist license had lapsed during the years of my using, I
began to work in rehabs after I had been clean and sober for a
little while—as a driver, a technician, and, later, a group facilita-
tor. After a few years, I was able to get my professional license
back and opened my private practice in Beverly Hills. Every
week I facilitate several recovery groups in rehabs and most
of my private clients are recovering addicts. It is my understanding that a psychodynamic approach with its emphasis on
uncovering (childhood) trauma can be too difficult and even
counter-productive with this population. I use a motivational
and cognitive-behavioral approach to treatment—as finding

hope and learning new modes of thinking supports the cognitive restructuring that takes place in early recovery.

I noticed that most recovering addicts don't really understand the mechanism of addiction and recovery—and, most importantly, that sobriety can be an option for them. In my groups I began explaining my understanding and experience of how it works. I put down in writing what I thought could be helpful and hand it out at each group. Clients loved the "Pearls for Your Recovery" as I called it. This book is a collection of these writings.

At this point I would like to insert some thoughts on human consciousness, which might clarify the importance of the spiritual path for recovery.

The approach of primitive man to the fulfillment of desire can be characterized by the maxim "conquer and dominate." It does look like we may be on the verge of a gradual transformation and ascend to a higher level of consciousness, where we move towards visualizing and materializing deliberately.

Humans are about 98% genetically identical to chimpanzees. Among other things, this means that our consciousness is a new feature of evolution. Anthropologists set the advent of our species at the point where we began to bury our dead, meaning that we had begun to imagine and conceptualize powers beyond the physical realm. The uniquely human aspect of life comprises our need to find meaning and purpose with the understanding of a possibly ongoing spiritual existence beyond this physical life. For millennia we have been speculating about invisible and intangible powers beyond, which would determine the circumstances of life and death. This inability to obtain certainty has given rise to fear and superstitious endeavors to influence and control fate. So far it has been futile, but we cannot let go of this quest.

People tend to view their own beliefs as truth, while devaluing others' beliefs as superstition. In the absence of verifiable certainty in these matters, a sense of discomfort arises and frequently becomes expressed in a felt need to convince, persuade, and even force others to acknowledge our beliefs as truth. Wars and crusades have been conducted for this purpose. Religious organizations have devised the concepts of heaven and hell as spiritual dwelling places in the afterlife, where life choices would be rewarded or punished forever, thereby attempting to enforce eventual justice, which appears sorely absent on earth. This shows the irony of utilizing the primate mode ("conquer and dominate") in spiritual matters.

In order to deal with the complexities of human life, we seek road maps in our desire to avoid getting lost. Guideposts are traditionally provided through one's family or community. In the modern world the traditional course of action, outlined by the social group of origin, has become much less influential. Ethnic or occupational groups, the youth culture, or association with other survivors of a troubling life experience have been sought out to provide a spiritual dwelling place via identification. An endless variety of behaviors express one's need to acquire a sense of belonging to some power or entity beyond the self. Some pursue idolatry through emulating public figures like rock stars, self-mutilate (with tattoos and piercings) in order to belong to a "tribe" (like a gang, for example), give up their individuality in order to "climb the corporate ladder," or spend precious life time on internet communication with virtual strangers—all in an attempt to avoid a sense of being alone in an incomprehensible world. Members can be "expelled" from these spiritual dwelling places through changes (for example, where the would-be member, upon outgrowing the youth-culture age, tries to ensure continued "membership" through plastic surgery). Ultimately, these endeavors wear thin, as they focus on the physical while leaving the spiritual need unaddressed (and the soul starves). The energy flow of this attachment to people and things can be visualized as horizontal—and tends to become depleted. One is left progressively exhausted and frustrated. When it becomes clear that the object of desire can never be attained on a permanent basis, a sense of futility creeps in.

Since existentialist and nihilist views entered the mainstream of thought, many people have become discontent with following societal norms and have ended up with a free-floating defiance against conventional attitudes, as expressed in the slogans "God is dead" and "No future." Without our having the ability to replace prescribed thinking with a sustainable superior solution, freedom of choice then becomes a challenge that cannot be successfully mastered. Permanent uncertainty and confusion creates persistent anxiety. The experienced discomfort is acted upon through excessive introspection, ruminations, obsessions and compulsions, which lead into a downward spiral of misery. When the "quick fix" of distractions, excitements, and intoxications wears off, people tend to feel lonely and lost in the midst of a life that appears futile and lacks the hope of a desirable future. This is the climate where emotional disorders and addictions can become inescapable conditions.

Addiction and mental illness are characterized by an inability to locate, access, and inhabit a spiritual dwelling place, at least not in a comfortable and continuous fashion. While biological and other physical factors certainly have a role in this, they can be influenced and altered through spiritual attitudes. It can be demonstrated that this spiritual dwelling place provides the guidance, safety, and hope we need. The interested participant can experience spiritual principles at work as they change physical reality. Thoughts and attitudes are creative and bring into being what we desire, fear, and believe—even if the mechanism is not thoroughly understood. It is suggested to utilize our power through a variety of "tools" and consciously direct our thinking to create a good life.

The spiritual path has been described as "seeking God" (as compared to religious convictions, which maintain that one knows the truth). An emphasis on connecting to a Higher Power, focusing on the present moment, adopting an attitude of gratitude and humility, and making oneself useful to others is offered as a solution through creating the experience of being worthwhile in a life that holds purpose and meaning. Here the energy flow can be visualized as vertical, where one is firmly grounded within while maintaining a receptivity to the spirit world "above," so to speak. Within this framework, fate can be understood as "God's will." Help and support for human suffering (from depression, anxiety, and/or addiction) can be obtained through acceptance of the status quo, or "alignment with the Divine Forces." It is understood that the creative life force (or God) flows through us with every breath we take, as we decipher, write, and complete our fate. Through "enlightenment," the path appears.

PART ONE

MY STORY

Is there something someone
forgot to mention to me?
—Lyrics from "Too Many Questions" by Sam Sparro

MY STORY

I HAVE ALWAYS LIKED FUNERALS. To be reminded that nothing really matters but the breath of life at this very moment. Good to keep the end in mind. A glimpse at the big picture. All our wishing, longing, trying, and worrying slides into perspective for a moment. Desire for attachments is futile. Pretense is a laughing matter. There was a time when heroin and alcohol helped me tremendously in my desire to forget about caring. Too bad that was a recipe for inadvertent deconstruction of all the good stuff that had come my way. The path of addiction took me to hell and back. Glad to be around to tell how I escaped the bottomless pit of despair that my toxic brain had created.

Utilizing the power of choice was never my forte. I was clueless. I used to go about things like a somnambulist, acting out on an endless string of feelings, for better or worse. The result

To Hell & Back

was a rocky life filled with love and excitement. Little by little I descended to a nightmarish place that became intolerable. There are various ways to look at my story and, depending on my vantage point and momentary circumstances, each narration can seem wrong, too. Let me just say, I have lived several lives, populated by adorable and colorful people, some of which have stayed around in spite of my various migrations (some got lost). They haven't necessarily done what I would have wanted. I forgive them now. While engaged with abandon in my wanton, careless, and forlorn dance on the edge of the precipice, I had hurt them, and I did have to ask their forgiveness. I wish I wouldn't have had to make it so hard for everybody, but that's how it was.

Instead of exposing my reader to a lengthy account of substance-induced predicaments, I'd like to relate one story sometime during the early nineties (the time frame is a bit blurry for me), which illustrates how I had disabled my mind. After having left my first marriage and my private psychotherapy practice so that I could use freely, I had taken my little son, Jesse, and moved back home to Munich, Germany (unencumbered with any considerations about his most loving and doting father in Los Angeles). My second husband, Markus, and I were struggling and working very hard in our hip little shoe store to maintain a lifestyle of being up all night, every night, with a generous and steady heroin supply. Hedonistic and exhausted as we were, we decided to take a trip to Goa, India, to take a little time out and get some strength back.

We were invited to stay at my girlfriend's house over there. Leaving the rough German winter behind for a few weeks, we arrived at this community of international travelers, who had sought out this place in paradise for its gentle, warm, and fragrant air, its lovely beaches, and beautiful, friendly people. Within a day we had located a spectacular source of cheap and excellent heroin to complement our Johnny Walker consumption. And so we continued in a daze of incessant intoxication.

We were told to rent a little motorcycle to get around. The traffic style on the local dirt roads was a bit confusing, since India had adopted the English way of driving on the left side of the street. The various participants from different countries weren't so sure of this, which regularly caused last-minute decisions upon eye contact with the opposing driver on how to proceed. We loved it and laughed at it, and shortly we had an accident. Markus's injuries were at his elbow, mine at my ankle. We didn't really care (heroin is an analgesic, meaning nothing hurts), went to wash the red sand off of our bloody wounds in the somewhat contaminated ocean water. The idea of antibiotic treatment or bandage honestly didn't occur to either of us. Markus's wounds began to heal (probably because they remained a little less dirty), but mine were continually exposed to more dirt and sand from the ground and the beach.

My wounds began to grow and fester. When sitting down, I would stretch my injured leg away from me so as to disown it somehow. When I joked with a friend about leaving traces in the sand from dragging the leg behind(!), he replied that soon I would leave a different kind of trace in the sand—of three indentations, from one leg and two crutches. I was a bit miffed, thinking that was a rude thing to say. Some days later we were walking on the street in the village and I had a moment's eye contact with a beggar who sat in brown and dirty rags on the sidewalk. Upon catching a glimpse of my foot, his eyes widened in fear (disgust?). I felt that he was thinking that there is something terrible going on that I am not aware of. This is when I finally (and reluctantly, I might add) consulted a doctor, who was seriously concerned about blood poisoning and saved my leg (and my life?) with a last-minute antibiotic treatment.

The foot refused to heal, but we still didn't find it apropos to return home. I remember vomiting many times out of the taxi window on our way to the airport (either from the heroin or from the gastro-intestinal infection I had picked up from eating food prepared on the ground at an outdoor full-moon party). We were too self-centered to even notice that we had disrespected my friends who had welcomed us so graciously. After being back in Germany, the oozing sores on my thickly swollen foot finally healed, but we had brought home yet another habit increase and proceeded to be even busier catering to these supply necessities. Naturally, things went downhill from there. We loitered around life, sliding blindly into impossible dilemmas, oblivious of reality and the consequences of our actions.

In the later years of my addiction, I struggled through some fierce suffering of my own making. I had exhausted my body and my resources. I had a moment of clarity, where I understood that heroin and alcohol are not my best friends, but essentially the source of my hell, the beginning and the end of my repetition compulsion. That's when I surrendered and gave up my defensiveness. I have been clean and sober since May 2nd, 1999, when I came back to Los Angeles and checked myself in to Promises Treatment Centers. Since my pursuit of happiness and oblivion with drugs, sex, and rock-n-roll had ended up in pathetic misery, I became teachable. They said, "All you have to do is be willing." I thought, "Hell, yeah, I can be willing. What do I have to lose?" So I did what it took and it worked.

In recovery I learned to say "hello" to people, and some other useful things, too. Through making amends, I got my dignity back. Meanwhile, I don't harbor bitter disappointments that come with unfulfilled expectations, and I have lost interest in blaming, convincing, or controlling others. My happiness doesn't depend on what they do, but on what I bring into my own little world today. It is essential to shift my attention away from past pain and on to what I want to get stronger. It's so much easier this way. In the process, I have learned to stand up for myself and don't have to hide behind an arrogant wall any longer. Through speaking the truth, my mind has emerged from the "fog" of vagueness and I found my voice. As I attend to life and overcome my weaknesses, I gain courage and self-confidence. When I show up for my people with a kind and loving attitude, I have a comfortable sense of self. I have come to understand that I have a disease of perception, which necessitates daily mental hygiene and spiritual guidance in order to get some mental clarity and balance. I couldn't do it without my twelve-step program.

My dozing spirit has been awakening. The spiritual path of compassion, forgiveness, and gratitude helps to avoid wasting my energy on fear and defiance. As long as I welcome my fate as the Divine will, acceptance replaces resistance. An attitude of gratitude helps me to let go of the struggle with myself and the world. I understand my task as a human being is to choose life, love, and creativity. I have noticed that my talents manifest when I am active and involved. The sincere intention of making myself useful brings purpose and meaning to my endeavors. Faced with a difficult situation, I imagine what the Dalai Lama or my cats would do and then I usually know how to handle it.

My life has become precious. I don't want drugs or alcohol, because I will not live in the darkness anymore. While I'm busy learning new things and bringing some hope and compassion to other recovering addicts, I can say with great content that my moods, urgencies, and self-destructive tendencies have eased. Doing the right thing is the key to a good life under the endless blue horizon. I listen to the wind. I am living in the light.

I'm walkin' on. I'm walkin' on. I'm walkin' on.

—Lyrics from "Too Many Questions" by Sam Sparro

PART TWO

ALCOHOLISM & ADDICTION

CATCH-22

ADDICTIONS HIJACK MIND AND VOLITION.

THEN I GOT TO CHOOSE.

KICKING IS A CATCH-22

—WHERE I'M SUPPOSED TO SEEK SOBRIETY,

WHICH ONLY A NON-ADDICT WOULD DESIRE;

—WHERE I MUST DEFEND AGAINST INVASION,

WHILE THE ENEMY IS INSIDE, INTERFERING WITH THE TASK

BY TAKING AWAY MY CONFIDENCE AND RESOLVE TO GO ON WITH IT.

I CAN SLIP INTO SOME LISTLESS VAGUENESS

—WHERE MY PERCEPTION IS BLURRED AND I FORGET TO LOOK FOR THE WAY OUT.

MUST REMEMBER TO HOLD ON TO THE COMPASS THEY GAVE ME,

EVEN IF I CAN'T SEE IT WHILE LOST IN THE FOG.

MEETING SOME PEOPLE WHO HAVE GONE BEFORE.

THEY SAY IT CAN BE DONE...

ALCOHOLIC / ADDICT

THIS BOOK USES THE TERMS *alcoholic* and *addict* interchangeably, although there are differences between the various forms of addiction. Different substances work differently for different individuals—therefore, in response to certain chemical reactions and experiences, we prefer certain substances over others. Also, please note that on a biological level it is irrelevant whether a drug is illegal, prescribed, or sold over the counter.

The Diagnostic and Statistical Manual of Mental Disorders, the "DSM-IV-TR," categorizes substances as follows (some other names have been added here in parenthesis):

- Alcohol

- Amphetamine (= Alpha-methyl-phen-ethyl-amine; other common names: Speed, Uppers; some common brand names: Adderall, Dexedrine, Ritalin; related compound: Methamphetamine = Methyl-amphetamine or Crystal Meth, Ice)

- Caffeine

- Cannabis (THC = Tetra-hydro-cannabinol, Marijuana)

- Cocaine (Crack, Freebasing)

- Hallucinogens (LSD = lysergic acid diethylamide, Acid)

- Inhalants

- Nicotine

- Opioids (Heroin, Morphine, Methadone, Codeine, Hydrocodone—e.g., Vicodin, Oxycodone—e.g., Percocet)

- Phencyclidine (= PCP, Sherm, Angel Dust)

- Sedatives (Tranquilizers, Downers, Hypnotics, Anxiolytics: Benzodiazepines—e.g., Ativan, GHB, Klonopin, Valium, Xanax; Barbiturates—e.g., Phenobarbital, Nembutal, Seconal)

- Polysubstance (use of various substances)

- Other (e.g., MDMA = Methyl-enedi-oxy-metham-phetamine—e.g., Ecstasy)

Some of us unknowingly become addicted to endogenous substances produced by our own brain—as in sex and love addiction, food addiction, gambling, or dangerous thrill-seeking activities. Living a conventional lifestyle, some people may rather use legal substances or prescription drugs. If you like excitement, you may seek the thrill of doing what is forbidden. If you suffer from pervasive anxiety, you may prefer opiates or benzodiazepines. If you suffer from agitation or ADHD, you may prefer cocaine, crack, or amphetamine for the "paradoxical effect" it can have (i.e., some people experience their effect as sedating instead of stimulating). If you feel depressed, insecure, or resentful, you may prefer alcohol to other substances. These days most of us are not purists—and combine several substances depending on their availability at the time. In trying to understand addiction, it is not very helpful to look for differences between liquid, solid, or powdery substances, or the mode of administration. The "ism" of alcoholism is not limited to the spirit in a bottle—it's more about an extreme and pathological reaction to reality, and the desire to escape.

Using the DSM-IV-TR as a reference, I would like to outline briefly the division of Substance-Related Disorders into two groups, depending on severity of use:

- Substance Dependence, or Addiction, is defined as "a maladaptive pattern of substance use, leading to clinically significant impairment or distress, as manifested by three (or more) of the following":

    1. Tolerance—"defined by ...a need for markedly increased amounts of the substance"

    2. Withdrawal—"manifested by ...the characteristic withdrawal syndrome for the substance"

    3. "taken in larger amounts or over a longer period than was intended"

    4. "persistent desire or unsuccessful efforts to cut down or control substance use"

    5. "a great deal of time is spent" on it

    6. "important social, occupational, or recreational activities are given up or reduced" for it

    7. "use is continued despite knowledge of having a persistent or recurrent physical or psychological problem" because of it

- Substance Abuse is "a maladaptive pattern of substance use leading to clinically significant impairment or distress, as manifested by one (or more) of the following":

  1. "recurrent substance use resulting in a failure to fulfill major role obligations at work, school, or home"

  2. "in situations in which it is physically hazardous (e.g., driving)"

  3. "recurrent substance-related legal problems"

  4. "persistent or recurrent social or interpersonal problems"

In this context I would like to add two other phenomena, which can occur in late-stage addiction:

- Adaptation—where the substance stops producing the desired effect regardless of the amount administered, potentially resulting in (accidental) overdose

- Rebound—where the desired effect is reversed; e.g., when benzodiazepines promote increased anxiety, or opiates incur hyperesthesia (i.e., increased pain)

Identifying the problem precedes finding the solution. Take an honest look at yourself and decide whether you ought to self-diagnose Substance Dependence. Whatever your "drug of choice," recovery entails abstinence from all mood-altering substances—unless you have a mood disorder or mental disorder, in which case you can benefit from professional help (i.e., consult a psychotherapist and/or psychiatrist). This is your chance to learn how to deal with your external environment as well as your internal world.

As a result of addiction, your brain has been chemically and biologically altered and responds differently to substances. The sweet memories you may have from the early days cannot be captured and re-experienced. It's over. You do not have to act out in a futile and tragic "Groundhog Day" repetition compulsion. Once you truly understand that—you can mourn these lost pleasures just like some people mourn their lost youth—and then you are free to move on.

As part of the recovery process, you will initially have to endure some discomfort—and then you can learn how to find serenity and peace. When you get your brain back, you can get a life. It CAN be done. There IS life after drugs!

ARE YOU A LITTLE GREEN FROG?

A S A CHILD I had a little green frog. Light as a feather, it could jump easily and elegantly. As it turned out, I was unable to procure flies in our city apartment and sadly decided to give it away to my girlfriend so that it could live. Her father proceeded to feed it thirty-six flies from their garden—on the first day. He might have meant well, but the frog died. We learn that quantity makes the poison. My little green friend could have had such a good life in their garden, but no. Clearly it didn't know when enough is enough. Frogs lack the ability to experience saturation. It is not essential for their survival while they live freely, because naturally they can't capture a deadly number of flies. My little green frog was like a car without brakes—it kept going at unrelenting speed and so it crashed. Maybe it was afraid of running out of flies again. I would say my frog had an addictive personality. What do you say?

During our evolution, while we had to survive in the wild, our ability to respond to saturation was never life sustaining. Dead prey gets a little icky when it's lying around bleeding into the dirt and it's somewhat cumbersome to begin hunting whenever you'd like a little snack. Stuffing ourselves while the supply lasted had its indisputable strong points.

Cancer cells, unlike healthy cells, also have this voracious and ultimately deadly greed going on. In fact, that is what defines them. Addiction is the relentless greed for more of something, due to a perennially incomplete sense of satiety, an inherent inability to experience saturation, contentment, or fulfillment. The healthy instincts of maintaining life are essentially replaced by a compulsive desire for a substance that would satisfy it but can't—because more is like the next fly for the frog—it won't reduce the sense of lack. Nothing is ever enough. Addicts keep on catering to their inner sense of lack—even when they are bloated like my frog when he was getting ready to burst.

SEEKING TO TAKE THE EDGE OFF

OUR BRAIN CELLS, the neurons, communicate with each other via neuro-chemicals such as serotonin, dopamine, norepinephrine, and GABA. Alcoholics seem to have unstable levels of these neurotransmitters, resulting in unpleasant states such as anxiety and depression. Recent scientific research considers the existence of an alcoholic gene, which causes a lack of dopamine receptors in the addictive brain. This would mean that addicts are predisposed for abnormal pleasure seeking.

Drugs affect the limbic system in the brain, the site of our survival mechanism, and thus change many functions, such as emotions, memory, learning, and appetite. Lacking dopamine receptors, the alcoholic tends to feel "restless, irritable, and discontent" and seeks "to take the edge off"—with some kind of self-medication like alcohol, heroin (or other opiates), marijuana (or other hallucinogens), cocaine (or other stimulants like crack), anti-anxiety medications (benzodiazepines, such as valium), and so on. In response to these chemicals, our brain chemistry changes beyond the desired effect—more or less permanently. The result is addiction; when the drugs wear off, the neurotransmitter levels drop even lower than before—way too low for comfort. Our brain becomes progressively more unbalanced, and we are compelled to drink or use our drugs of choice even in spite of life-threatening circumstances.

Addicts also seek relief behaviorally by trying to numb emotional pain through endorphin release. Endorphins are natural painkillers, producing a state of well-being. Pain, stress, and/or excitement stimulate the brain to release endorphins in an attempt to re-establish the equilibrium. Addicts try to get that through other forms of addiction as well, such as sex addiction, gambling, fighting, excessive working out—anything that promises tension relief, either instantly or after temporarily increasing the tension. Unfortunately, for the alcoholic/addict no amount of activity along these lines is ever sufficient.

In recent years, non-addictive medications have been available to support sobriety. The most commonly used are antidepressants of the SSRI (selective serotonin reuptake inhibitors—e.g., Prozac) type, which maintain higher levels of serotonin. SNRIs (serotonin-norepinephrine reuptake inhibitors—e.g., Effexor) act upon two neurotransmitters and can help some alcoholics to feel less depressed, anxious, or obsessive-compulsive.

Alcoholics Anonymous (AA) suggests that alcoholism is a spiritual, mental, and physical disease. Spiritual support and guidance through AA, plus psychotherapy, plus medication can be used for treatment. Breathing exercises, prayer, and meditation on a daily basis promote relaxation, which counteracts fear and agitation. It does take some effort, but alcoholics can find permanent relief—as long as they don't change their mind halfway through the process of recovery...

HEDONISM

BRAIN RESEARCH SHEDS SOME LIGHT on self-destructive addictive behavior, which can seem so incomprehensible. Addictive drugs mimic brain chemicals, which provide pleasurable feelings, and our brain adjusts. As we develop a tolerance, we need more and more drugs to feel O.K. When we don't have our drugs, we feel horrible—and we experience withdrawal. This is addiction.

The brain releases dopamine, the stuff that makes us feel calm and content as a reward for life-sustaining behaviors; for example, when we respond to hunger with eating, or to thirst with drinking, or to sexual desire with sex, or when we try to protect ourselves from a threat with the "fight-or-flight response." The addictive brain reacts differently to events and drugs. To drugs, our survival system responds with an extreme dopamine surge, which alters our brain chemistry—so we feel the need to get more, and more, and then more. As a result, the "hedonic set point" rises and we experience our needs with life-threatening urgency until all our actions are devoted to an insatiable hunger for pleasure while we may not care that our life is in danger. Avoiding pain and seeking pleasure, which is originally pro-life, becomes essentially pro-drug.

Addicts have an extreme reaction to things. It starts out with "hedonism"—meaning that seeking pleasure and avoiding pain is our most important pursuit. We begin to take drugs because we want to alter the way we feel. On drugs, remember, we evaluate and learn things differently, and so we create a "perceptual bias." We think we "have to" do things that are socially unacceptable and we'd rather hide that from others, and so we get defensive. When we feel ashamed we attack and blame everybody else, and so we create different experiences and events as we go along. We can't show up for our responsibilities and so our life becomes frustrating, confusing, and scary. We aren't able to follow through with our promises, and people tend to be frustrated with us. We can't deal with it, and we can't face people anymore. When we run out of drugs, we become flooded and overwhelmed with agitation, anxiety, depression, and despair. Therefore, we feel that we must avoid acute withdrawal at any price, and procuring a steady drug supply becomes our first priority. Being preoccupied with obtaining and using drugs, our view of reality becomes skewed and things get chaotic.

At this point we have a lot of problems and chaos to deal with, so we really need to get high. By the time we become desperate to maintain our drug supply at any price, we are living in constant chaos and despair. That's when the drugs usually quit working. Now, no amount of drugs provides the needed relief, and the real-life problems become overwhelming. Joy and happiness are a distant memory, as if from another life. There is no more oblivion from despair. For the "hope to die drug addict," it's all about survival for no good reason. Some addicts overdose when they can't stand the relentless daily struggle anymore. Some of us surrender and choose recovery…

INSANE IN THE MIDBRAIN

NO MATTER HOW YOU LOOK AT IT, addiction is not a smooth ride. We are struggling with something that's located right in the center of our brain, which makes it impossible to get rid of. However, recovery is an option and that's really all you need to know. Besides, it is a whole lot easier to live sober than to live with a toxic brain. For one, you can think clearly and so you can take care of things and make decisions that are good for you. You can get a life. That's good.

In addiction and early recovery, your prefrontal cortex, the brain area of reasoning and decision-making, is somewhat under-active. You can't think straight and so you may be tempted to do stupid things. As a result, you feel like you don't know how to "do life" and you get overwhelmed with mundane tasks that healthy people don't have to think twice about. It takes about ninety days for your brain to reset itself to a more functional level, which is really not so terribly much time, all things considered. This is why you need a lot of guidance, support, and encouragement during this time, so you won't feel so lost. Alcoholics Anonymous provides all that and you get a chance to change gradually and gain some self-confidence and clarity.

Now to the midbrain, the survival part, the site of the "reward system," where it's all about the amount of dopamine available between the neurons in order to feel good. Normally you get a little extra dopamine boost as a "reward for good behavior"—meaning activities that are relevant for survival. Doing the right thing makes us feel good. For addicts, this part is a little fickle, and we don't get nearly as much dopamine as we like, which is why you have been self-medicating for so long and neglected everything else. In late addiction, nothing matters but catering to the dopamine supply. Unfortunately (and I say this with all my heart), the continued use of addictive substances results in an under-supply of dopamine, and that's not a good thing—the longer you use drugs, the less they work (as you very well know).

Withdrawal is not a smooth ride, either. Getting clean reduces the available dopamine even more, which feels miserable and there is no way to get around it. However, this stage is time-limited and you will gradually get better, every day. Everybody does, even if it doesn't feel that way sometimes. Watch out for stress during early recovery, though. You won't be able to handle it well at all, no matter how cool you think you are. It's very important to feel safe. That's why rehabs can be so helpful by giving you some "time out" from the chaos you created.

Once you recover, you will find out that you can deal with your problems one step at a time, one day at a time, and with the love and support of other recovering addicts. In sobriety we learn to be kind with ourselves and let others show us how to have a good life.

SELF-SOOTHING

ALCOHOLICS HAVE INEFFICIENT self-soothing mechanisms —when we get excited, we don't know how to calm ourselves down. We can get agitated for any or no reason, and then we stay that way for an extended period of time. We may experience it as fear, anxiety, anger, or resentment or perceive it as a nagging desire for diversion and excitement. No matter what we call it, we can't relax; we are irritable, restless, and discontent. "Normal" people also get agitated, but they can calm themselves down, usually within minutes. For us, it may take hours to downward regulate such a highly charged emotional state, and that can be difficult to endure. So we feel the need to take the edge off with some substances. It's just too uncomfortable for us too much of the time. Alcohol initially has the sedating effect we seek, so we continue to drink to feel even better. However, after the first one or two drinks, the opposite begins to happen—we get agitated and dis-inhibited, with unfortunate and embarrassing results as we act out while our impulse control is set on "off."

Many alcoholics also use other substances in need of a break from their unnerving internal state, such as benzodi-azepines, barbiturates, or synthetic opiates, which are highly addictive and cause much worse withdrawal symptoms than alcohol does. With poly-substance abuse, the addictive process becomes multiplied and complicated—as the toxic brain becomes progressively incapable of producing the desperately sought-after pleasure. The reversal of these damaging and enduring alterations in the body during withdrawal is particularly difficult and lengthy.

Alcoholism is a chronic disorder that requires ongoing treatment. In recovery we acquire a way to deal with our alcoholism. Twelve-Step programs provide tools for feeling comfortable in our own skin, for some of us for the first time in our life. We can exit the downward spiral of destruction and eventually establish some serenity and peace.

AVALANCHE

Most people don't go there.
Some can't get it started, no matter what they do.
Under certain circumstances,
one little step can unleash an avalanche
with such power
that it destroys everybody in its path.
We never know.

Unconscious thoughts and convictions
about our own unworthiness or the futility of life
can make us go where we should not go
or follow those we should not follow,
and break loose an avalanche no one can stop
until it has run its course.

They say… what we don't remember,
we are doomed to repeat.
I am asking you, as the survivor of such a calamity,
will you remember?

PART THREE

TOOLS FOR YOUR RECOVERY

Sometimes, when we are caught
in a net of unhealthy desires,
we think that we are on a path to happiness.
Such self-deception always leads to suffering.

—from *Teachings on Love*, Thich Nhat Hanh

BE YOUR OWN GOOD MOTHER

ANY ADDICTS AND CO-DEPENDENTS come from dysfunctional families where we were not encouraged when we felt insecure or comforted when we made mistakes. Some of us were told things like, "You are no good; you will never learn; why can't you ever do the right thing?" We have internalized some of these experiences into our subconscious memory. This means that years later our inner voice may continue to repeat these verbal memories like an automatic recording. We may not even be aware that this relentless inner voice is fueling our misery. Perhaps the people who said these things have passed on, but their words continue to harm us, and we remain with feelings of insecurity, inferiority, hopelessness, and/or anxiety. In recovery we learn to identify and discard dysfunctional inner verbalizations and replace them with thoughts that encourage a positive self-image. As a result, we begin to develop confidence and self-esteem, while self-hatred and self-destructive tendencies wither away.

Easily and gently acknowledge what is going on inside your head. Allow it to be whatever it is—without judging it or trying to stop it. Be still and get to know yourself. Writing it down can be of help. You will realize that you don't have to identify with this inner voice any longer. In fact, when you are listening to your "inner sadist" you end up feeling miserable. Once you are aware of this, you can replace such negative self-talk with a phrase that works for you. Create some positive affirmations that you would rather repeat to yourself, such as, "I can make mistakes and learn from them," "I deserve a good life," and "I am allowed to be happy today."

Imagine for a moment being a little child recovering from a severe illness. Imagine also being the good mother talking to that child. Then say to yourself what a good mother would tell you. "Don't worry, my love, you are guided and protected. Tomorrow is another day and you will feel better." When you realize that you have made a mistake, talk to yourself as your own good mother: "No big deal, next time you will do better; everybody makes mistakes. I love you anyway." When you notice that you have slipped into self-loathing, go back to this exercise and tell yourself what you would tell a child whom you love. These cognitive techniques have been used successfully to change habitual thought patterns that trigger a fearful or hopeless emotional response. Give yourself permission to be wherever you are on your life path, wherever you need to be for this phase, for however long it may take. Be accepting of temporary discomfort during your internal process, and the pace of your development, especially if it seems less than perfect. Let yourself be who you are right now, without demanding that you be different, better, smarter, faster. It's not necessary. Be gentle with yourself as though you are dealing with yourself as a little child. Although this exercise may seem silly to you, you will notice that it works. Why don't you give it a try?

Remind yourself on a daily basis that change will occur by making recovery your first priority—everything else will follow. You heal as you raise your awareness and integrate more useful contents into your thinking process. Be attentive to learning about yourself and your life. Be kind and patient with yourself. Healing and growth must take time. Whenever troubling thought patterns return, embrace them as a part of yourself that still needs some patience. Resort to prayer. Some of us survive early recovery by praying whenever necessary throughout the day. We all struggle as we go through life. It's not about the pursuit of flawlessness; it's about engaging in life and having experiences. Give yourself permission to go forward at your own pace even if it appears slow, just like a child on his first bicycle supported by training wheels. Your time for outgrowing this stage will come.

DAILY MENTAL HYGIENE

MY CATS SPEND A LOT OF TIME grooming themselves (sometimes they feel a little damp from their tireless hygiene activities). However, after returning home from vacations, we notice that our cats' grooming behaviors have slacked—they look deplorably shaggy. They seem to neglect themselves when they feel neglected. In a way, alcoholics remind me of my lonely cats— daily grooming doesn't appear to be high on their priority list, either. In fact, they behave as though they don't care all that much about personal hygiene, housekeeping, and other areas of their life that require regular and consistent attention.

Alcoholics Anonymous addresses this lack of care with the slogan "Dress up and show up" no matter how you feel— hardly a necessary reminder for all other adults. The idea is that functional participation in our own well-being, while directly promoting positive results all around, indirectly counteracts depression by feeding the message back to our subconscious mind, "Since I am taking care of myself, I must be doing well." We end up feeling good, or at least better than before. One of my clients complained about her trash piling up as she couldn't get herself to take it out frequently enough. Upon completing the "homework" assignment of taking her trash out on a daily basis and reporting back to me when she had done it, she felt a lot better about herself. This may not seem like a big deal, but it sure felt like a great encouragement to her to experience herself moving forward in the right direction—after having been "stuck in the bondage of self," where she couldn't get herself to do this little task in spite of the fact that not doing it made her feel bad.

Every day take a little step forward toward better self-care, whether you "feel like it" or not. It does get much easier after the first one or two steps, as you remember that you were able to do so before—and felt empowered. Climbing a mountain also begins with one step. The first step starts a self-reinforcing mechanism—you become encouraged by your own movement, and eventually you get to the top.

BREATHE AND MEDITATE

YOUR SPIRIT IS ENERGY. Wherever you put your attention, your energy follows. Every choice you make, based on faith or fear, directs your spirit and has energetic consequences. Your thoughts create feelings, which in turn influence what you think—a feedback loop. In response to a perceived threat, your nervous system prepares itself for the so-called "fight-or-flight response." The operative word here is *perceived* (see also the topic "Perception"). If you are encumbered by "unfinished business" from your past, you may be experiencing threats where there are none—on constant alert for no reason. Through maintaining a state of anxiety or anger, you deplete your energy. It is as though you step on the gas pedal in your car without putting it in gear. You waste energy without going anywhere. Eventually the gas tank will be empty and the car will break down.

When you're agitated, your breathing is shallow. Agitated states, such as anxiety or anger, are physiologically incompatible with relaxation. By changing your breathing pattern to calm, deep breathing, you send a different impulse to the brain, counteract agitation, and create relaxation instead. The breathing exercises (see the topic "Breathing Exercises") require that you count as you attend to your breath, which interrupts your obsessive fear-producing thoughts, as the mind can only hold one thought at a time. By repeatedly going through this process, you learn to pull your spirit back from upsetting thoughts and begin to cultivate and bridle your powers. When you are accustomed to this technique of creating peace for yourself on a daily basis, you can add some visual imagery (see the topic "Visual Imagery") to deepen the process. With more experience, you will be able to meditate without these tools. You will learn to be still and find comfort and joy within yourself by merely attending to your breath.

BREATHING EXERCISES

TOXINS AND HABITUAL OVER-EMOTIONALITY tend to create an imbalance in your physical energy. When your system becomes depleted and exhausted from the consistent stress, generalized anxiety or chronic anger can eventually cause illness to manifest. With the following breathing exercises, you can balance your energy when you can't seem to relax. If you have never had any experience with meditation, this is a great way to get used to sitting in silence by yourself in and attending to your breath. The required counting will naturally interrupt any obsessive mental content. You can support your recovery by making this a daily morning practice and end up feeling much more comfortable and calm throughout the day. You could also add some visual imagery (see the topic "Visual Imagery").

1. Find a comfortable seat in your house, possibly near a window where you can see the sky. Sit erect with a straight back (almost like a puppet on a string) and support your lower back with a pillow, if necessary. Lower your shoulders (which tend to be raised when you are anxious) and let your hands lie loosely in your lap. For a solid sense of grounding, keep your feet placed squarely on the floor, or pull them up on the seat and cross them, if that seems more comfortable.

When you are ready, close your eyes, take a deep breath, hold it for the count of seven, and then release it easily and evenly. Take a few normal breaths and repeat this until you have done it seven times.

2. Sit comfortably as in the previous treatment, close your eyes, and take a deep breath. Exhale slowly, and when all the air is completely out of your lungs, hold it out for the count of five. Then breathe in and out easily a couple of times. Repeat until you have done it five times, then breathe normally and put the entire procedure out of your mind. This treatment is purifying and, believe it or not, is very helpful in treating the common cold if practiced in the early stages of infection!

If you inhale and hold seven breaths,
your oxygen will be completely circulated
through your blood system,
and you shall not need what you are longing to have.

—Yogi Bhajan

PRAYER MAGIC

WHEN I WAKE UP IN THE MORNING, I pray. I thank God for all the good in my life. My gratitude list goes like this: "Thank you that I am clean, sober, and healthy, that I can see and hear, walk and talk, breathe and show up for my life, that I am not in pain, that I can do everything. Thank you for the love and joy in my life. Thank you for everything." I list all good things that come to mind. "Please show me the right way and give me strength, courage, and health to bring love and joy will shall be done. Please protect me and my people (I list them by name)."

When I fill my heart with love and make my entire day a prayer, I feel content, whole, and complete. When I realize that I have slipped back into worrying, I pray. If I am angry with some-body, I pray for them. If I worry over something I think I need or something I fear to lose, I pray. Prayer instantly calms me down and relieves me of my sorrows. Do I know who is listening? Absolutely. *I* am listening. Is a Higher Power listening? Nobody knows. We are meant to live the mystery. Atheists believe there is no God. This is a belief, too. I believe that my prayer addresses another dimension, a dimension where the answers lie. Does it matter whether it is so? No. Prayer helps me to create some serenity for myself when I need it. Good enough. I don't need to know how it works. For me, it's sufficient that it does. The spiritual path is about seeking God, not about having found Him.

There is more to it, though. Our thoughts can manifest material things. I have been able to manifest things through visualization and prayer. It has changed my life more than I can say.

Visualize whatever it is that you want, then give it to the universe. Concentrate on the joy of having what you want—that way you won't manifest the wanting. Please understand that you must not get attached to the object of your desire—the magic happens as you turn it over to God and let it go. Prayer is non-material, so it is easier to manifest non-material things, such as sobriety, faith, prosperity, or being surrounded by love—which then create material things, as well. If you hold on to anger or fear, you create more powerlessness—as you waste your power over objects beyond your control. Concentrate on gratitude, acceptance, and your connection to your Higher Power—and you will see that prayer is so very empowering.

MY TWO FAVORITE PRAYERS

Morning Prayer:
"Whatever, God" or
"I welcome everything. I push nothing away."

THIS ATTITUDE OF FAITH, acceptance, and surrender allows you to align yourself with all that is. Turn your life over to the care of God (instead of trying to control what you can't). See what's up. Be open and curious, just like when you are starting to see a movie and wonder what it is going to be about.

Evening Prayer:
"Thank you, God" or
"I am grateful for my life."

With this spiritual stance of gratitude, you experience your life as precious—like having a bag full of jewels. Enjoy it, use it to your benefit, take care of it, and share it. It is a spiritual law that you must claim your blessings in order to keep them. So list all of your blessings and make the best with the cards you have been dealt.

BE STILL

S IT BY YOURSELF in silent meditation, close your eyes, observe your breath, and attend to your internal process. Easily notice the stream of consciousness that makes up your inner world. Give it your attention and patience, and let it be until it slows down. Let go of judgment, and allow feelings and thoughts to come and go. Listen to the voices inside, so they do not have to yell so loudly anymore. The process of getting to know your truth will enable you to feel O.K. in the midst of silence and turbulence. It is through being who you are that you find meaning in your life. What could be more interesting than getting to know yourself?

Buddhist teachings suggest that we attend to our own inner world. By practicing this technique of allowing our inner process to be just the way it is, we realize that we can observe thoughts, feelings, and events without necessarily reacting to any of it. We are taught to allow everything to be there—easily and without trying to change anything. This awareness in itself empowers and transforms us.

Sitting in silence promotes awareness of our "true self." Having grown up without sufficient nurturing and useful guidance, some of us felt unlovable and unimportant. If our survival required that we compromise our sense of self-worth for the needs of others, we may have lost touch with our sense of self. We got stuck in a reactive mode, ever in fearful anticipation of other people's actions and reactions. Being dependent and seeking to survive adversity, we may have become numb to what seems less urgent—even if that is our own self. We constructed a "false self" and eventually got confused about who we are. As a result, life came to appear unpleasant and futile.

Regular practice of meditation can be very helpful for correcting our perceptions. Instead of automatically reacting to other people, anxiously appeasing the demands of life, and habitually trying to avoid discomfort, we can give ourselves the space to observe our experiences. We can learn how to quiet down, even in the midst of disquiet and turmoil. We discover that emotional pain is not unbearable when we accept it for this moment, instead of demanding that it be gone instantly. It is only when we stop running from ourselves that we find peace.

Be still for a little while to quiet down—every day.

A MEDITATION ON LETTING GO

SIT COMFORTABLY with your legs crossed. Lay your hands in your lap, palms up, keeping the left hand easily in the right hand. Sit upright with a straight spine, like a puppet on a string. Close your eyes and keep a half smile. Notice your breath for a little while. Know that your breath is forever connecting you to life. Imagine the energy flowing through you as limitless, purifying, loving, Divine life energy.

A meditation on the five aspects of your being:

- Say to yourself, "I am my body and I am aware of it." Your body is your vessel to dwell in. Become more and more relaxed and aware as you easily notice your breath flowing in and out. Let it take away your tensions. Enjoy it.

- Say to yourself, "I am my feelings and I am aware of it." Notice the feelings you have—fear, anger, sadness, whatever it may be at this moment. Allow it to be there, notice where it is located in your body, then allow it to flow out of you with each breath you take. Be kind with yourself. Remember love and go back to the half smile.

- Say to yourself, "I am my mind and I am aware of it." Notice the thoughts you are having. Allow them to be there, then take your attention back to your breath. Be kind with yourself. Go back to the half smile.

- Say to yourself, "I am my perceptions and I am aware of it." Notice any sensations you have of the world beyond your immediate being. Allow them to exist, and easily take your attention back to your breath. Go back to the half smile.

- Say to yourself, "I am my consciousness and I am aware of my awareness." If any of this is confusing, allow it to be that way for now, then go back to attending to your breath and your half smile.

Please do not expect anything like a perfect "performance" from yourself. Just sitting with yourself in silence and attending to your breath is enough. Don't force a time limit on it, either. If you keep doing this meditation on a daily basis, it will grow on you. You will become accustomed to disengaging from fear and pain and replacing it with serenity and peace.

VISUAL IMAGERY

FOR BEGINNERS, meditation can feel a little odd. Starting with breathing exercises can help you get accustomed to sitting with your eyes closed, experiencing yourself "being there." As mentioned, the counting that goes along with it will disrupt your obsessive thinking, and the deep breathing will help you relax. When you're ready to add more to your meditation, visualize ONLY ONE of these images:

- I am a big, strong, beautiful cherry tree. My roots are firmly planted in the ground, spread out deep and wide, supplying me with an abundance of all the nutrients I need. I feel joy about being alive by just being who I am—night and day, in the sunshine, in the rain. I can weather any storm. I offer my luscious green branches for singing birds to sit and build nests on. I have millions of lovely blossoms. I grow big, fat, juicy cherries—and offer them freely to whoever comes to me. I don't have to do anything. Just being here is enough. I am precious, just being who I am.

  This image is especially helpful when you feel anxious, driven, or disconnected from the Source.

- I am a funnel for Divine energy to flow easily and effortlessly through my being. I don't have to produce anything at this moment—just being open and aware of my nature to channel loving energy for the benefit of all creatures. This is what gives me joy.

  Helpful when you feel greedy or needy.

- I see myself from above like my own guardian angel, hovering over me with big, beautiful, fluffy wings— watching over me and caring for myself.

  Taps into your inner wisdom when you are in doubt about what decision to make.

- I am a big, beautiful bird, flying gracefully through the endless blue sky. Gliding on wind currents, I don't even have to flap my wings. I enjoy feeling the cool breeze on my belly and the ecstasy of being with the elements—weightless and free. When I am hungry, I swoop down elegantly to catch a fish. It's my nature to be swift enough. I want my mind to be clear—so I can enjoy life, find a mate, build a nest, and show my adorable little fledglings how to become a great flier and catcher like me.

  Great exercise to support your sobriety.

- I am sitting at a river on a heavenly meadow. I look around and enjoy this enchanted surrounding. It's grand. When I feel resentment over some past hurt, all I have to do is put it in a basket and send it down the river. I watch it disappear as it goes down around the bend.

  Great for letting go of self-pity or a desire for revenge and becoming receptive to a sense of peace.

- I got what I want.

  Imagine yourself having whatever it is that your heart desires and being grateful for it. Feel what it is like to be in that spot, then send this film to God. Your wish is a command to the universe to be fulfilled—as you let go of its fulfillment. It works. I have done this more than once.

POSITIVE AFFIRMATIONS

Watch your thoughts, for they become your words.
Watch your words, for they become your actions.
Watch your actions, for they become your habits.
Watch your habits, for they become your character.
Watch your character, for it becomes your destiny.

—Mahatma Gandhi

THE QUOTE ABOVE ASSERTS just how powerful your thoughts are. What you think determines how you feel, speak, behave, and how the world reflects back to you. It can happen that you inadvertently create a life you don't want. Putting your attention on fear always creates suffering. Never concentrate on losing, needing, or blaming! Instead, put your attention on loving yourself and giving love!

Use the "magic of the spoken word" to interrupt and counteract fear-based obsessive thinking. Choose three or four positive affirmations, and repeat them to yourself thirty times a day for three weeks—until they become "automatic." The positive affirmations will replace your old negative automatic thoughts, because the mind can only hold one thought at a time. Notice the immediate calming and soothing effect. What are you waiting for? Start right now!

These are my favorites:

★   I am guided and protected.

★   I am at peace with everything.

★   I am allowed to be happy today.

★   I bring love and joy wherever I go.

★   I welcome everything, I resist nothing.

★   I am exactly where I am supposed to be.

★   I am aligned with the Divine Forces today.

★   I never have to do anything that I cannot do.

★   All I ever have to do is to show up for today.

More affirmations to choose from:

•   This is my life.

•   This moment is mine.

•   I am right here, right now.

•   I am a Divine child of God.

•   I am grateful to be sober today.

•   I have the right to live my truth.

- I am perfect, whole, and complete.

- I am strong. I am smart. I am enough.

- I am lovable and beautiful the way I am.

- Happiness is a result of love coming out of me.

- All of my experiences are useful; I learn from each of them.

- My recovery is like a young tree, growing stronger every day.

IT IS WHAT IT IS

FOR TODAY, I CHOOSE TO LIVE LOVE,

HAVE SOME FUN, LEARN A LITTLE, AND TAKE IT EASY.

I DON'T HAVE TO TRY SO HARD.

IT IS WHAT IT IS.

I FORGIVE MYSELF, MY MOTHER, MY FATHER, AND EVERYBODY ELSE

FOR EVERYTHING.

I LET GO OF ALL BLAMING SO I CAN FEEL LIGHT AND BRING LOVE.

IT IS WHAT IT IS.

WHEN I LIVE IN ACCEPTANCE, LIFE IS GOOD AND I AM AT PEACE WITH WHAT IS.

ALL OF MY EXPERIENCES MAKE UP MY LIFE.

THERE ARE NO MISTAKES.

IT IS WHAT IT IS.

I AM ON MY PATH. EVERY STEP TAKES ME TO THE NEXT ONE.

I AM MEANT TO LIVE MY TRUTH,

AND YOU, TOO, MAY BE WHO YOU ARE.

I AM ALLOWED TO BE HAPPY TODAY—AND SO ARE YOU.

A LIFE LIVED IN FEAR ISN'T MUCH FUN

Anxiety does not empty tomorrow of its sorrow,
but only empties today of its strength.

—Charles Spurgeon

T HE FUNCTION OF FEAR is to prompt us to react to an immediate danger so that we may prepare to defend ourselves or flee. Chronic anxiety has nothing to do with anything immediate at all. We fear that we won't get something or that we'll lose something. Meanwhile, we ruin precious life time that we could experience for what it is—a moment in time without knowing the future. While we focus on uncertainty and vulnerability, we worry and feel nervous. Our behavior reinforces our fears—our perceptual bias and irrational thinking become more and more engrained. Fear feeds on itself as fear-based behaviors become habitual and take up more room in our inner world.

Constant fear is toxic, destructive, and potentially deadly. In spite of all the evidence to the contrary, we live as though the things we fear are really happening. As we try to avoid discomfort, we avoid life, procrastinate doing things, and withdraw from people or imagined enemies. Meanwhile, we cater to an inner enemy, which eventually renders us dysfunctional as we become paralyzed with our own hyperactive reactions to imagined events. Most of the things we worry about never come to be.

Make a conscious decision to walk through your fears. As you experience yourself overcoming unpleasant feelings, you realize that you can do it, that nothing terrible happens—and you reinforce your strength. Next time around, you remember that you were able to walk through it. As long as you live, you can build new habits that work for you. Spiritual guidance can help you adjust faulty perceptions and replace fear with hope and faith. You can overcome your fears and create a fulfilling life—if you take some action.

- Every human being knows anxiety states in reaction to threat. This is nothing special or embarrassing.

- Animals experience anxiety as well, but only briefly, in response to an actual threat.

- Humans can imagine threats where none are present.

- The human brain doesn't differentiate between an actual and an imagined event.

- During an anxiety attack, the object of one's fear is experienced as real.

- Alcoholics tend to overreact to situations, get anxious easily and frequently, and stay that way for prolonged periods of time.

- Fear is a physiological condition of readiness for fight or flight (AKA aggression or withdrawal) in order to secure survival—and, as such, consists of utmost tension, which is the opposite of relaxation.

- During such a state, adrenalin floods our system, suppressing all vital functions (such as digestion, breathing, etc.).

- In order to address anxiety physically, it is necessary to promote relaxation on a physiological level—by feeding back to the brain the message "the danger is over."

- As a result, the body will go back from hyper-alertness to relaxation.

- This can be achieved with a brisk walk for ten (or more) minutes, which loosens muscle tension and furthers deep breathing. This may need to be repeated once or twice per day.

- Breathing exercises are an excellent tool (during walking, as well). Repeat whenever necessary.

- Finally, a little visualization, where you imagine that your head has an opening on top (just like a baby's fontanel)—where golden, loving, Divine, healing energy flows in and proceeds to cleanse your whole inside of the dark-gray fear energy—until your whole inside is glowing warm and golden. Then change this color to the pale lavender-pink color of love, until you become a "ball of love energy." Feel the joy.

- Then do some affirmations.

Fear creates mountains. Faith moves mountains.
—Author Unknown

UNTAMED MIND

IF YOU ARE AGITATED and/or anxious, you probably didn't get some desire satisfied, or you are unsure about the solution to some problem. If things have not been working out as you expected, this does not mean that you must force your will onto something or somebody. It does not mean that you have to look at your fear as an enemy that you must eradicate instantaneously. It does not mean that you must act out at all. It could mean that you have been pursuing an error, that you haven't been on the right path. Look at your fear as a messenger from your subconscious—as your intuition speaking to you. Look for guidance and clarity. Allow yourself to calm down naturally and let your fear speak to you.

Going through life with an untamed mind is like dealing with a bunch of wild horses—balky, shying, and runaway broncos. Your physical sensations, thoughts, and feelings run in all directions. If you want to get somewhere, you need to collect and bridle your horses. Then you can put them in front of your wagon and let them pull you to your destination.

You can tame your mind by exerting some mental discipline. Make it a daily morning routine to be still by yourself for a few minutes and experience who you are. Raise your awareness to your inner process and feel your feelings—it won't kill you. When you concentrate on the feelings you are experiencing, notice where they are in your body, and allow them to be there. Easily notice their existence, and embrace them as an expression of your life force. You'll be surprised to notice that emotional pain is not "unbearable"—unless you try to make it go away instantly. Take some time to explore the thoughts behind your feelings. Write down what the problem is, what you feel and think about it, what the other person did, and what you did.

Have a soothing spiritual book handy to do a little daily reading—so you get a different perspective and avoid tunnel vision. Do some positive affirmations. Go for a walk. Say a little prayer and ask for faith and gratitude. Taming your mind is a process, just like domesticating a wild horse, but it's necessary if you want to get anywhere.

WATER, B, C

OUR SURVIVAL IS SUSTAINED through fresh air, water, and nutrition—and not through cigarette smoke, alcohol, and heroin chic. Who would have known?

Our internal environment, which consists mostly of water, relies on a regular and sufficient supply of fresh water to function and detoxify. If you are a good alcoholic/addict, you hardly ever feel thirsty, and so you drink little or no water. This seems to be the result of our focus on drug-seeking that has replaced the normal life-sustaining behavior (which is programmed in the dopamine system in the midbrain). In our disease, we drink alcoholic beverages; in early recovery, we drink coffee and sodas. What this means is that our body turns into something like a warm, poisonous, and eventually lethal pond—a breeding ground for disease. As a result of this toxicity, you may suffer from all kinds of pains, as well as intestinal and other dysfunctions.

In addition to this, certain substances deplete us of nutrients. Alcohol and sugar deplete us of vitamin B, a lack of which can cause severe nutritional deficiencies with a variety of dangerous, disturbing, and possibly painful consequences. Memory impairment in chronic alcoholism and Korsakoff's disease are due to serious vitamin B deficiency. Vitamin B replacement in early recovery can reverse some of these conditions. As a smoker, you might want to supply yourself with a high dosage of vitamin C—since nicotine depletes you of vitamin C, which can have dangerous consequences, as well.

It took me years to identify dehydration as the cause of my abominable headaches. The most important thing you can learn here might be: DRINK WATER and a lot of it, eat lots of fresh produce and unprocessed foods, and take vitamins—on a daily basis.

PART FOUR

RELATIONSHIPS

All that we are is the result of what we have thought:
it is founded on our thoughts, it is made up of our thoughts.
If a man thinks or acts with selfless thought, joy follows him,
as a shadow that never leaves him.

—Buddha

RAFT PEOPLE

LET ME TELL YOU a little story about my relationships around the time when I got sober and unknowingly shifted addictions from substances to a man.

We were laughing. We were having fun. We were kicking holes into our boat… The boat had begun to sink. I tried to fix the holes; I tried to patch them. I did everything I could. My husband and my son were in the boat with me. We loved each other so much. I was bailing water out with a bucket all the time. Other people were drifting by on their own boats, enjoying the ride, but I couldn't even take a little break for fear that the boat would sink. My husband kept collapsing from the relentless struggle, getting a break from time to time. While he was out, I had to bail for both of us. The water kept rising slowly, at first up to my ankles, then up to my knees, and finally the water was almost at chest level.

Something had to be done. I saw it clearly: No matter how hard I was working at it, the holes were too big and too many. The boat was beyond repair. Either we would sink or I would drop dead from exhaustion—whichever would happen first. In any case, we could never again have a normal ride on this boat. At that instant, I knew we had to jump into the cold water and swim—each of us on our own. I jumped, knowing it was the only way. I had to find faith.

I remember swimming in the cold water. I was keeping in contact with my husband and my son, relieved to see that they were able to swim on their own. Far away in the distance I made out the shore. There were sunny sandy beaches, pink houses, and palm trees to be seen. Friendly people were waving at me to come over. I managed to swim there. I was so happy. I was saved. I was able to build a little shack and get my son, too. I had lived through so much; I had learned so much—and I began to be of service to other shipwrecked people. I showed them how I survived so they would be able to do it, too.

Meanwhile, my son had become a man and had started to live his own life. I was lonely and I met a man. He was sweet. He called me "Baby"; he called me "Precious." He told me that he loved me and would never leave me. At first I didn't really believe him; he seemed too sweet. But then I dropped my guard—and he went back to his rainy island up north. I loved him, I missed him, and I didn't want to live without him.

I left my son in the little house on the pretty island and, on a raft, followed this man. When I got there, I saw that he was on a raft, too—another woman's raft. He had been on other women's rafts his whole life, and they were tagging along. They were lonely, looking for love. He called them all "Baby" and "Precious." He had promised love and happiness to them all—and they had believed him, just like I had, and when he left, they were too heartbroken to move on. Through abandoning everybody, he could be sure that he would never ever feel abandoned again like he had felt when he was a little boy and lost his mommy. He thought loyalty meant being loyal to everybody at the same time, acquiring women like jewelry and feeling like a wealthy man.

He had lots of children and grandchildren and a wife, all jumping on and off rafts, trying hard to follow him with every new woman. When they arrived at the raft he was on, he smiled and jumped off. They had been following him from raft to raft for so long, they were tired and felt lost. They had wanted to have a house of their own with him, as did all of the women. He could never say "No" to anyone—so he kept hurting everyone.

That was what I saw after I got there. I wanted to leave, but I was exhausted from my long, long journey. I had been working so hard for so long to get my life back together after having destroyed my own boat. I didn't find the courage to leave again. He said he was old now and tired and his knees couldn't do all that jumping anymore. He wanted to retire. I tried to have faith in him and our love. He wanted to change. He wanted to be a good man. His presence was irresistible to me. The nights in his arms were bliss. But I wasn't able to forget his betrayal, his deceit, and his lies. The poisonous snakes of distrust and resentment were growing inside me. I was smiling less and less. I began to see that he couldn't deliver what I needed to do for myself. Had I been stupid to believe a man's words more than my own intuitions?

We struggled—with each other and with ourselves.

Most of his children were grown, but had never learned from their parents how to build a house of their own, except for his oldest daughter, who was mad with resentments, overwhelmed with trying to hold everything together. All of his people—his women, his children, his rafting buddies—were angry with me. They thought that through me he was finding steady ground under his feet, and they felt left behind. He said I was sent from heaven to save him from drowning. Sometimes I felt like I was in the wrong movie. Neither of us knew how to handle things.

He said that he knew how to have a home, take care of a house, and that he wanted to do that with me from now on. So I found a beautiful little house for us to be happy in. I was on foreign ground. I kept on looking at it—was the ground under our feet being washed away? Had we built on sand? I was running out of faith, out of patience, and out of confidence. I had used it all up. I had been given the grace to manifest my dreams, and gotten stuck in an all-exhausting struggle again. Had I misused my powers?

I remembered that I had been loving and kind, and had had patience and understanding. Where had all that gone? I was angry, resentful, exhausted, dejected, and so very tired of the consequences of my own decision. My light had become so dull; you could not see it anymore. Gone. Couldn't find a niche for myself on the rainy island. How could I be useful to other shipwrecked people? I used to guide them with the pictures I drew in the air. Had I lost my grace by putting my spirit into wanting one man's love instead of shining my light to everyone around me? Had I lost my gift?

Once again I had to take a plunge into the unknown. I realized that I had to find my own home—on solid ground. I had to take my spirit back from desires and illusions. I was told to stand erect in my pain, walk through my fear, and take care of myself—and when I did, I finally began to flourish…

LOVING A PORCUPINE

FEAR CAN BE A POWERFUL and destructive force in the life of an alcoholic, prompting us to cling to drugs, sex, and rock-n-roll in order to avoid looking at ourselves. In early sobriety, some of us are tempted to shift our addiction from substance to romance. We may fall in love with another newly sober alcoholic, who might be busy trying to escape his own discomfort and consequently proceed to sacrifice everything for a little relief. We may seek safety through holding on to another person who cannot even provide it for themselves. This kind of relationship may provide some oblivion of self—through distraction and drama. However, because of the typical vulnerability during this phase, loving someone else who is also unstable and unpredictable can be like loving a porcupine. We hurt each other—and we cannot help it. In trying to forget our own fear and pain, we could end up trading it for someone else's fear and pain. The focus shifts from seeking spirituality to seeking physical contact with a lover. This is not the recipe for serenity and can interfere with the ability to enjoy our newfound sobriety.

Usually, it doesn't work. The distraction can make change impossible, but some of us stubbornly insist on holding on to old behaviors—just like I did at the age of ten at my summer vacation on the Romanian Black Sea beach, when I had just learned to swim. My old lifesaver had a hole and was deflated, but I would not go into the ocean without it. Even though I knew that it could not carry me anymore, I liked the illusion of support. I continued to use it anyway for a while, until one day I was willing to leave it behind. At first it felt a little strange, but then I noticed that it was fantastic to get out from the heat into the beautiful cool water and swim freely, unencumbered and unrestricted in my movements.

As I stayed sober for a while, I noticed that my fear level stayed low as long as I desisted from futile attempts to avoid risk and uncertainty and replaced self-limiting and self-destructive behaviors with the willingness to change, learn, and grow. It can be so sweet to give up the compulsive need to hold on to old strategies when it's time to let go.

A CO-DEPENDENT RELATIONSHIP

Jane thinks: "No one loves me."

She looks for someone who would need her.

She finds Joe and thinks: "I'm lonely. You're here."

Joe drinks and doesn't take care of his problems.

Jane tries to understand. She tries to help.

Joe likes it and begins to rely on her.

He ceases to do things for himself and for her.

Jane begins to feel burdened and unloved.

She resents him for using her

and blames him for her problems.

She demands: "If you love me, change."

She complains and she nags.

Joe doesn't like to be criticized.

He does change: he resents her and withdraws.

Hardly the change she had in mind.

Jane fears losing him and becomes clingy and whiney.

She cries: "I hate you! Don't leave me!"

This ruins his mood.

He wants to have some fun. He tries to get away.

She is heartbroken.

She thinks: "No one loves me."

DRAMA

I F YOU ARE UPSET about something or somebody, consider taking a moment to open your eyes. Look around you: if there is nothing happening outside of your head, it's drama—all *in* your head.

We are meant to use our time and our power for our life's purpose. Sometimes, though, we lose the right path. We may feel scared when we notice that we are lost and don't know where to turn. We may feel like blaming others, lashing out, trying to force them to admit that it's all their fault. We may feel like creating some drama—acting out in anger to hide our fear. Is it going to be useful to spend our time deciding whose fault it is that we took a wrong turn? Think! Use your mind! What can you do to come out of the thicket and see the light?

When we sit around expecting others to subordinate their own needs to ours, we get resentful. When we don't show up for our life, we feel miserable. When things don't happen as we think they must, we feel depressed. So we create drama to externalize our inner discomfort. While we attack those before us, we may forget for a moment that we feel bad about ourselves. It provides some distraction, but won't address the cause of our distress. With us lost in the thicket, the problem is not our fear but the fact that we are lost, and denial won't get us out. Imagine a movie where the hero is lost in the jungle and he closes his eyes and blames his mommy…

Walk through your fear. Stand erect in your pain. Address your problems one at a time, one day at a time. Make yourself useful today. Bring some kindness and compassion to the people you see. They might need some encouragement to go on. If you do this every day, your life will get better. And so will your self-esteem and your mood.

LOVE AN ALCOHOLIC

IN ACTIVE ADDICTION

WE LEAVE A TRAIL OF HEARTBREAK AND DEVASTATION

TOO PAINFUL TO CONSIDER.

THROUGH OUR SELFISH PURSUIT OF OBLIVION,

WE CAUSE PAIN TO ALL AROUND US.

IN EARLY SOBRIETY

WE LOOK AT A PILE OF BROKEN DREAMS——

THAT IS OUR LIFE.

IN OUR PEOPLE'S EYES

WE SEE FEAR, DISTRUST, AND RESENTMENTS.

THE HEALING POWER OF RECOVERY

CAN PROVIDE A CHANCE FOR A DIFFERENT LIFE——

A GOOD LIFE——

IF WE LEARN TO LET GO OF BLAMING

AND ALL THE OTHER WAYS

WE HAVE TORTURED OURSELVES AND EACH OTHER

AND FIND THE WILLINGNESS TO FORGIVE.

SEX & LOBSTER

ECAUSE WE ARE SOCIAL ANIMALS, relating and bonding is of utmost importance to our survival. If we live in fear of abandonment, we tend to cling obsessively just as soon as we connect. Consequently, our relationships tend to not work out well. Out of our fear of being lonely, we become lonely. Fear-based behavior promotes suffering as we create what we fear. This can be so painful that we feel too vulnerable to get involved and eventually avoid intimacy altogether. Some people think they don't want to pay the price of commitment. They turn to "casual sex" with strangers. I compare this with hunger for food: Most of us would agree that freshly prepared home-cooked food is preferable to fast food. Both kinds of food satisfy hunger and can be enjoyable. Processed food is mostly void of the nutrients we need to sustain us, and in the long run we end up deprived of what we really need. We may look fat while we are starving inside.

The same goes for compulsive sex-seeking. Alcoholics tend to be irritable, restless, and discontent—so we look for relaxation any way we can get it, and we can get addicted to whatever feels good for a minute. In our disease we seek instant satisfaction, and some of us pursue love or sex indiscriminately. Since sexual satisfaction is relaxing, one wants more. What one finds is the quick thrill of sex with a stranger, ultimately meaningless as it leaves the deeper need for intimacy unsatisfied. Afterwards, the sense of loneliness aches worse than before. You will find that "normal" people in loving and committed relationships are usually not incessantly preoccupied with sex.

In recovery we realize that we have been paying a high price for our impulsive acting-out. We see that our deeper need for relating and connecting needs to be satisfied without damaging our self-esteem. We learn how to take better care of ourselves, choose behaviors without shameful consequences, and begin to build the kind of life we want to be in.

THE PERFECT MAN

- Are you a woman dreaming of a man who will "make you happy"?

- Have you been looking for the perfect man who will take care of you and make your problems and pain go away, but found men who caused pain and problems?

- Have you believed men's seductive words at the first night in a bar, telling you how precious and special you are?

- Do you take a man's sexual interest as proof that you are beautiful?

- Have you been hungrily seeking everlasting unconditional love in breathlessly quick sexual encounters with indifferent strangers whose faces or names you can't recall?

- Have you been rushing from one sex object to another so you can feel powerful for a moment, as you interpret a man's sexual desire for love?

- Have you disguised your need for intimacy by presenting yourself as cool and aloof, while you quietly died of loneliness inside?

- Have you had sex with a man to try to hurt another man, who doesn't even care?

- Have you done everything and more to keep a man who has been hurting you?

- Have you craved sex with your man so you would forget his betrayal?

- Have you accused and blamed and attacked your man to cover up your fear of being abandoned one more time?

If you are an alcoholic woman, chances are you'd have to say yes to some of these questions. Sex and love addiction and co-dependency go hand in hand with alcoholism. As long as we are in our disease, we don't know how to care for our emotional well-being and physical safety. Alcoholic women live danger-ously. Being involved with alcoholic men introduces more dangers.

Driven by desperate neediness, we compromise our sense of self-worth and don't care much about asserting boundaries. This makes us easy prey for predators, who may be violent—before or after we blame, attack, or act out in self-destructive ways to hide our fear and shame.

As you fantasize about symbiosis with every new guy, you are setting yourself up for disappointment, pain, and possibly abuse. You probably know this by now, but you may not have wanted to acknowledge that your man's flaw is not the problem.

The flaw lies in your wish, or, more precisely, in your insistence on having your wish come true, against all odds, and certainly against your experience. You fear and expect lies, betrayal, and pain, while tenaciously holding on to old attitudes and habits— out of fear. As a result, you keep repeating the same experiences with every new man.

The truth is that love lies within you, the power lies within you, and so does the solution. You don't have to sacrifice your whole life to a fixed idea that has been causing your suffering. Once you get to the point where you refuse to live in this repetition compulsion any longer, you will see that you are free to live your dream of love and joy. It begins by busting out of your defensiveness and giving yourself the chance to heal.

S&M

WHEN PEOPLE HAVEN'T FOUND the safety, love, and satisfaction they need, they may opt for intensity. Intensity provides extreme experience. Danger or threat prompts our brain to release adrenaline and we get excited. Pain stimulates endorphin release and we feel euphoric, which can be a powerful physiological high.

Those of us who have endured a childhood of lack, deprivation, and abandonment may feel the desperate need to avoid being lonely, at all cost. Any attention seems better than having been abandoned and forgotten, and being hurt becomes preferable to being ignored.

Love-starved children develop a deep-seated conviction that they are undeserving of love and respect. Abused children grow up with the understanding that love equals pain. In response to abuse, a child's sensitivity is harmed. They may eventually become numb and/or callous and seek the extreme stimulation of pain. Often this is accompanied with other substances, to alter their sensations even more. This can become an addiction in itself and, like all addictions, can become more severe over time. An adult survivor may end up despising what could be a comfortable and loving relationship while misinterpreting mutual abuse and humiliation as intimacy. Being mistreated or "punished" is accepted and even sought-out because it is familiar and expected, while a gentle and kind partner may be rejected as boring or despised as weak. Painful interactions validate low self-esteem and are used habitually to act out internal tension.

The masochistic role of surrendering one's free will while being at the mercy of another can elicit a sense of power through the ability to endure pain without being broken. Meanwhile, the violence can escalate, spiral out of control, and cause serious harm.

The sadist has given up on true love and won't risk being vulnerable anymore. They settle for domination, where they attempt to ensure their control and physical safety. The sadistic role of inflicting pain and humiliating someone else can feed the illusion of being superior and powerful in order to forget about feeling helpless and unhappy. Too bad it doesn't work out that way. We cannot get rid of our own pain by inflicting it on someone else. Both the sadist and the masochist remain victims. What they want most is to be paid attention to, and they sacrifice their soul and integrity in the process.

In early recovery from alcoholism, patients may feel tempted to self-sabotage by shifting to other addictions and self-defeating activities in order to return to familiar terrain, thus perpetuating their suffering. If any of this sounds familiar, you might want to seek out psychotherapy so that you can uncover your true self underneath the masks you have been wearing. Sobriety is about finding freedom from compulsive self-destructive games. You may need to develop self-love, self-esteem, and self-respect so that you learn to assert safe boundaries and feel comfortable within your relationships. In order for you to have a good life with some serenity and peace, it is very helpful to work a good recovery program with close contact to other recovering addicts for support while you discover how to let go of the roles you have been playing your whole life. This is the time to heal your pain and sorrow.

BIRDS OF A FEATHER

I N EARLY RECOVERY we tend to associate with other recovering addicts. We have survived the same calamity, and just like the survivors of the *Titanic*, we feel a common bond. This can be a lifesaver since at this point our other relationships are often encumbered or altogether destroyed. We can have some fun and also get the support and comfort we need.

In your discomfort, you may feel tempted to attach quickly to someone who understands you and shares your experience, in the hope of getting some nurturing and alleviating your pain. Some of us feel so uncomfortable with ourselves that we "quiver" to get sexually and/or romantically involved at this point, and take whoever is before us without much discrimination. This usually turns out to be a mistake, because sharing the "survival mode" is not sufficient to sustain a relationship. At that stage, everyone else is needy, just like you, and has nothing to give. As a result, they add more pain and confusion, the "perfect" ingredients to trigger a relapse. It can be devastating to be involved with someone who is going to relapse, which you cannot prevent, while you are barely holding on to your newly found lifesaver.

Chances are you have plenty of experience with dysfunctional relationships—you may not need another one. Addiction has been your mode of relating and you haven't learned yet how not to relate addictively. So you risk switching addictions from your drug of choice to a person. A co-dependent attachment is just another addiction—you cannot have any control over it. It always causes suffering—because all of your energy is focused on getting something from the outside. It can even become more powerful than the addiction to substances, especially if your childhood needs for love, nurturing, and safety have never been met.

Early recovery is a magical time, accompanied by enthusiasm that spills over into our new relationships, and can make us overlook incompatibilities. It has been called a "pink cloud" and "honeymoon period," where a world-famous film diva can fall in love with a truck driver. At this critical phase in your life you are filled with hope and compassion, but you are still vulnerable and your recovery requires all of your strength. This is the time to get to know who you really are underneath the surface commotion of your addiction, to quit acting out on impulses, and to learn how to be yourself. After a little while, when you cease to over-identify with the addictive side of your personality and develop your sense of self, you will be able to find "your kind of people." Give it a chance!

FIGHTING WITH MONSTERS

Whoever wants to fight monsters must be careful not to turn into one.

—Friedrich Nietzsche

I F YOU LOVE AN ALCOHOLIC, you are suffering. "Wet" alcoholics can be desperately difficult to deal with. They can be most aware of your weak spots and willing to use the scalpel on your self-esteem with snide precision—to hide their helplessness behind hurtful and threatening hostility. Your alcoholic has been deceitful, manipulative, disrespectful, and disloyal. They have also been sweet, loving, and all-around adorable. They have blamed you, betrayed you, lied to you, and apologized for it all, only to stab you again before your wounds were healed. You are exhausted from a never-ending battle with forces beyond your power.

You may be utterly confused about what to believe and what to do. You may feel guilty, ashamed, and hurt—but unable to withdraw from the exhausting intensity of this relationship. You may feel tormented about your responsibility and your need to save them and yourself from destruction. You may feel unclear about your part in their disease and recovery, trying to make sure that they are safe, and get viciously attacked when you try to help—and you may still want to save them. Once you truly understand that a drowning person will drag you down with them, you can give yourself permission to do what's best for you. If they won't swim or hold on to a lifesaver, there is nothing you can do. If you feel hopeless, you may be "hitting bottom" with the futility of this endeavor. Ultimately, no one can control another's wish and fate, even if they give their own life for it.

The twelve-step program of Al-Anon uses the term *loving detachment* and suggests pulling back from all behaviors that are focused on controlling an alcoholic. Alcoholics Anonymous teaches us to "carry the message, not the alcoholic." Alcoholics have a warped perception and are torn by a conflict of ambivalence. This is why they "bite the hand that feeds them." They may resist their rescuers like enemies, while loving their enemies. If you try to point out the "blind spot" of their denial they will turn against you, and you may become angry, resentful, and unhappy. You may get stuck trying to "make them understand" or help them against their will, and lose yourself in the process. This is the dynamic that will pull you down—if you won't let go. An alcoholic who doesn't want to get sober won't get sober, no matter what the consequences are. While they are drinking, they cannot change. You can change, though, and get your life back. They may come around when they are sick and tired of being sick and tired, or when they have exhausted all their resources and "hit bottom." Whether you are an addict or love an addict, or whether you're a "double winner" (both), keep in mind that recovery cannot be forced upon another person. It's an inside job.

FAMILY FUN

You may remember a difficult childhood within a dysfunctional and/or alcoholic family. Dysfunctional families tend to be rigid, disrespectful, intrusive (lacking functional boundaries), and keep secrets. Out of shame, subjects like incest, addiction, and abuse may be denied and not revealed to outsiders. This kind of family teaches that it is preferable to stay in pain rather than get help. Children end up full of fear and confusion—feeling different from everybody else—while being lonely and too insecure to speak the truth. In order to cover up vulnerabilities and low self-esteem they learn to resort to denial, deception, and various acting-out behaviors. If a family member gets the chance for help and begins to change (against all odds), these families tend to resist and sabotage the change for fear of being left behind or out of embarrassment about "having their dirty laundry aired in public," especially if substance abuse is involved.

While you are in early recovery, a family visit may be difficult for your sobriety—if your family tries to recreate the old intimacy via destructive behavior patterns. You may feel criticized, attacked, threatened, or punished, and lose your hope—which is still like a delicate flower at this point. The verbal and nonverbal messages you get from your folks may tell you that you are not free, and that your new friends simply don't know how (sick) you really are. Never believe anybody who tells you that you don't have a chance to be happy—no matter what you did, or what they did to you! Close contact with your Higher Power, sponsor, therapist, and the recovery community is most important as a daily reminder that you have begun a new life. This connection, support, and understanding will help you to claim the right to take care of yourself.

Here are some pointers to keep in mind whenever your sobriety and hope are being challenged:

- Make your well-being and your sobriety your number one priority.

- Talk to other recovering addicts; read, write, and— above all—pray.

- Don't explain or defend yourself. You don't have to.

- Don't engage in painful old habits such as fighting. You don't have to.

- Anytime you feel like it, say: "This is not good for me."

    - Or "I don't want to do this." Remember, you are free and have a choice.

- Or "I don't want to hear (talk about) this right now."
- Or "No (thanks)." Your family does not have to understand (if they don't want to).
- Or "I have to go now." You don't have to dwell in drama anymore.
- Or "Let me think about it." Stalling can give you a moment to regain your stability.

Don't be over-confident. Threats of abandonment, hand in hand with engrained old habits, are powerful. You can stay sober, though, and you will end up feeling empowered—and so much more useful to your family when you recover.

ASSERTIVENESS

ALCOHOLICS TEND TO BE CO-DEPENDENT. We like to focus on others so we can avoid looking at ourselves. We do things for them, and demand that they change for us. We may be confronted with people who try to take advantage of us with manipulations, where they try to make us feel guilty by calling us selfish. We sacrifice our own well-being and expect to be appreciated for it. We have difficulties being honest, for fear of not being loved. We may avoid confrontations, things don't get resolved, we feel resentful, we nag and blame, and the other person ends up resentful, too. We may be under the impression that we are loving, when in reality we are needy and judgmental. It can get confusing to do the right thing.

In recovery we put our own sobriety first, and we learn to be kind and accepting. It is important to create a positive emotional environment for ourselves. We must let go of resentments or we may not want to stay sober. So we must learn to be assertive. This means that we stand up for ourselves and speak our truth—we say "yes" only when we mean it. My grandmother used to say, "This is not good for me," when something didn't agree with her—she knew to be kind and assertive at the same time. If we don't set clear boundaries, we end up feeling powerless, angry, and/or depressed, and turn to (self-)destructive behaviors when we cannot stand it anymore.

Your need to avoid confrontation is not kindness, but weakness. Let go of your incessant need for approval and your fear of standing up for yourself. People treat you as you teach them to treat you. If you are afraid of setting limits, others may become exploitative and/or abusive. For example, if somebody asks you for money and you don't feel right giving it to them, say "No" if that's what you want to do, and you won't have to be resentful. You don't always have to explain why. They may not wish to understand, and they may not have to. Faced with the choice of them being angry or you being angry, it's better when they are angry and you have your money in your pocket. It's empowering and liberating. If people treat you in a hurtful or disrespectful manner, it's on you to stop them. If you won't stand up for you, who will?

It is beautiful to be giving and helpful to others—only if it is voluntary. It's sweet to be kind from a position of power, but it's bitter when we let people walk all over us. Remember, recovery is about being happy, joyous, and free.

PART FIVE

THIRTEEN
ALCOHOLICS

1. LARRY BREWS

I WAS A GOOD LITTLE BOY, good little boy. Too bad I was too little then. I got teased. I excelled in school, sang in the choir, did this and that. When I became a teenager, I felt humiliated that I was still skinny. I hated my body. It was pretty much expected of me to display athletic abilities, but, being so small, I could never do that. In order to distinguish myself, I became a bad boy. I was trying to escape reality. I did get a little jail time here and there (in reality, that is).

Eventually I got to go to college in Illinois, and then dropped out to "party." I made my own beer in a crock and became popular for it. Over time I did graduate from college—and also to amphetamine and psychedelics. Meanwhile, I had a little family, became disillusioned with academia, and wanted to become a working class hero, whereupon we left for the West Coast. We

stopped overnight in Denver and stayed there for thirty years—
some of us, anyway (the marriage didn't last). I made pottery
for a living, which provided money for beer and drugs, and I
was hip. I was no longer skinny. I felt attractive and got some
attention. The world was my oyster, or so I thought. Whatever I
desired, I took. Looking back, I have to admit that I had become
uncaring, callous, and sociopathic by then.

Some fellows came into my studio who looked like responsible and compassionate men. They seemed to have their life
together and also time to drink. They were firemen, and so I
became a fireman, too. Things happened and my second wife
left, somewhere around the time when I tried to run over my
neighbors and their friends with my car in a drunken stupor. My
captain took me to a twelve-step meeting. I wanted to say that I
am not an alcoholic, that I just need to control my drinking, but
came to admit at that meeting that I am an alcoholic. I have not
had a drink or drug since that day—12/9/1979.

I live by a simple formula: I get up in the morning, hit the
ground running, kick ass all day, and leave the results up to God.
I have finally become the man I always wanted to be. I am per-
fectly comfortable in my own skin, in my own home, in anyone
else's home, and on the street. I have confidence in God with
complete abandon, and I find it more exciting and edgy than
the bad-boy lifestyle ever was.

2. RACHEL SEEKS ABUSE

GREW UP IN AN ABUSIVE HOUSEHOLD. My dad is an alcoholic and my mom was never there. I was incested from the time I was a little child, mostly by my dad and stepdad. My sparse childhood memories are not worth remembering.

When I found drugs and alcohol, they provided the oblivion I needed. They helped me forget my life—until using and drinking stopped working.

I got sober at thirty-two (on 1/14/2007) and saw that all of the intimate relationships I have had in my life have been abusive. In years of therapy I realized that I sought them out to play out my past pain. My father never loved me like a father—when he got near me, he injured and terrified me. I found out that I feared real love, because that would mean that indeed my whole childhood was loveless, and so I sought out men who would hurt me and I constantly tried to make them love me the way I thought they should.

I really had no idea what love was. In recovery, I am learning that love is not pain. It is only by staying sober and getting my brain back that I am able to cultivate enough self-esteem and self-love to want a man who loves me. Slowly I am able to learn love by being loving to others. Only by staying sober am I able to stop the cycle of re-victimizing myself through judgment and criticism. I am not torturing myself anymore. Only by doing affirmations that remind me that I am lovable and a Divine child of God and by helping others unconditionally am I able to achieve this.

In sobriety I have my first loving relationship. I have learned to tolerate and accept love from my boyfriend and in return love him for being exactly who he is, even if I don't like all of his decisions all of the time.

3. LUCAN BREAKS SOME BONES

GUESS I WAS ANGRY A LOT without knowing it or showing it. My mom is a party woman. She likes to drink a lot. Sometimes she was not around and my sister took care of me. It didn't bother me because I was so young. I didn't have my feelings there, really.

We had moved from Los Angeles back to Munich, Germany, and somehow we had "lost" my dad—or at least I did. I was ten when my dad, whom I barely remembered, called and promised that he would send me a ticket to visit him in Los Angeles. I waited and looked in the mailbox every day for months and months before I gave up. From then on I didn't really want to talk to him when he called, thinking, "Yeah, right, tell me another stupid story." Also I had forgotten how to speak English. My mom told me that he eventually did send a ticket some years later and I went. I don't remember it, but this is what happened—no one came to the airport to pick me up. I waited for about fifteen hours or so until the immigration officers had located my dad's girlfriend over the phone. She eventually came to get me. After that vacation, I had no contact with my dad for fourteen years and he moved; I never knew where he was.

I began rollerblading when I was sixteen. It changed everything. I became really good at it, never minding the occasional broken bones. It was fun. Being sponsored by sporting equipment companies, I saw the world for free and met other professional inline skaters. We went out every night to party. That's when it started. I began to drink and smoke pot. Every once in a while I drank more, more, more—until I needed a drink in the morning to get rid of my hangover.

Through my success in rollerblade competitions, I was invited to participate in the world championship in Switzerland. My Polish friend and I were the only two Europeans who made it to the top ten. So we partied all night, but woke up on time for the final run. We smoked a joint or two before the run until we fell asleep again and missed the finals. Still makes me mad. Stupid is what that was. Our sponsors were not happy and quit sponsoring us. Nobody wanted us after that. I dropped out, found a new friend, and began to snort cocaine day and night. I broke some bones—fighting. I stole. I went to jail. I was desperate for what seems like a long time.

Meanwhile, I knew that my "substitute parents" had been sober in Los Angeles. Their son, my best childhood friend, had moved back to L.A. as well. His dad had offered me to come to his rehab and even pay for my flight whenever I would want to go. I never did. Somehow I could never make it to the airport. I kept calling them, until one day my mom just grabbed me and took me to the airport. That's what they tell me. I can't remember anything about all that.

I have stayed sober since that day (9/27/2004) and I thank God every day for that. I wouldn't be here without the people who loved me and never gave up on me. I am very grateful and will always be there for them. My life is wonderful now. I love to be sober. I love to work. I don't feel scared and broken anymore. Ever. Although my mom and my dad are still the same people they were then, I am no longer trying to change them. I am glad that I have changed. I am busy building a life for my wife and son. Who would have thought that I would ever have such a good life, where people respect me and, even more importantly, I respect myself?

4. LIZ IN A BOTTLE

MY FATHER WAS VERY VIOLENT and my mother cried all the time. They are still together. Being the oldest kid, I never knew what I was supposed to do. I became an artist to create beautiful and colorful things.

My drinking didn't start until much later, in my mid-thirties, because of various disappointments when the fashion world failed to provide the stability I needed. Early on I excelled at art—it was my escape and only happiness that gave me peace. I had pretty fabrics and ribbons as a child, got art scholarships in high school, and had a concrete purpose in college—I was going to be a fashion designer. I would take twenty units so I could graduate sooner and start my life. At twenty-three, I sold to Nordstrom with my own label. I opened my "Hat Gallery" when I was twenty-seven and had numerous write-ups in the glossy fashion magazines. French and Japanese magazines came to interview me. But the fashion industry is short-lived and cruel. I began to have difficulties reinventing myself. I went inside a bottle and stayed there for twelve years. I had learned to drink before, but my goals for myself had been stronger than my desire to punish myself. I was in an M.F.A. program for painting when I realized that I had such a drinking problem.

I had been exposed to recovery through friends at school. My friend said, "Alcohol will always be more important than any relationship." When I realized that I was a mess, I decided to stop drinking. I believe in God. So I had faith that He could remove my desire to drink. And that's what happened. I was able to graduate and I am presently learning to love myself even if I'm not famous. It's kind of neat how things that were messed up in our childhood become ways to save ourselves.

5. GARY, THE FAILED BIG SHOT

MY MOTHER THOUGHT I WAS SMARTER and more handsome than anybody, and she doted on me. My father was a traveling salesman and not around much. My sister was largely ignored. Being cradled in a symbiotic relationship with my mother was good until I had to measure up with other kids at school. It got me crazy and I began to act out for attention. A large part of my life became about making it O.K. to be me.

I was happy to be me for a while when I first started using drugs. I did them all. I knew nothing about myself, although I had been going to psychotherapy for a few years. Meanwhile, I had a couple of successful careers. I achieved some fame and with that came money, which made me successful with the girls. I was generous with drugs, but also mean-spirited and demanding. I think I was getting even with the girls for not liking me as a child.

Eventually I obtained everything I thought I wanted, but it was never enough. The height of my disappointment and insanity came when we had been up all weekend at my friend's house in the hills, behaving badly with numerous girls. Walking around in a stupor, after a night of debauchery, I went into his closet to look for more drugs and found a gun. I brought it out to the pool and said to my friend, "Let's kill one of them." I scared him and he didn't really want to hang out with me after that. From there I moved on to heroin full time in order to be less crazy. I began to isolate in my beautiful, big house in Malibu Canyon and, strangely, took up scuba diving. I thought it was so smart that I was doing that. Down on the bottom of the ocean, high on smack, sitting and watching colorful fish swim by.

At this time, my career as a film producer was over. After my successful first movie I had been living large, but apparently I can't handle success. The second movie barely got finished. I was a joke. The studio I was producing this movie for kidnapped me to an island off of Florida for a forced detox. Eventually everything was taken away and I was discarded.

At forty, I was a failed big shot living in my parents' house. I would drive around in this beat-up old car that someone had given me and visit the places I had lost. My life was just despair. I hit bottom. Then, on a Sunday morning in November 1982, I had a spiritual awakening. Leafing through the *L.A. Times*, I saw an article about a new self-help organization that had just started. I called the number and proceeded to tell the guy who had answered what a big shot I was. He hung up on me. I drove immediately to the address listed in the article, and there was a meeting going on. I identified with these people and I felt comforted. Also, I saw something in there that I really wanted. They were laughing. It was funny. I was so filled with shame and fear that I didn't talk to anybody, but I did go back the next day. After about a month, a guy who remembered me stood at the door and grabbed me by the shoulders as I tried an early exit. He wouldn't let go of me until I looked up from the floor. He said, "You're gonna be alright. If you have a desire to stop, we have a program that works."

I have been clean and sober since January 1983, and I am a totally different person today. I'm not afraid anymore, at least most of the time... I think I have finally become the person I was meant to be. I have two beautiful children who have never seen me loaded and crazy. I feel so lucky living in a marina right by the ocean. All the gifts that recovery promised, I got them.

6. SHAME SHAME SHAME

A PRIEST RAPED ME inside the confessional box when I was eight. My parents were with me at that church, but they never realized that this priest was so interested in my beautiful little skirt. I couldn't say anything, just wanted to leave, but they were standing around forever talking to people. So I went to sit in the car, and I sat there alone for a very long time before we drove home.

I remember that my dad used to have nude parties at our home. I drank beer foam since I was three and we gave it to the cats, too, to watch them stagger around. There was also some incestuous stuff when I was three or so. I have memory flashes of my father fondling me. He was a psychiatrist and told me that he was doing therapy with me. I remember counting walls, windows, or tiles, trying to multiply the numbers to distract myself.

I didn't like that I was stuck with my brother, who was a baby then. He was a nightmare. He kept on biting into the drinking glasses until they broke and he would bleed everywhere. I never knew what to do about it, and then I would be blamed for it. I was always blamed.

My dad was twenty-five years older than my mom. He died when I was ten. My mom was drunk then and she is drunk now.

She didn't care much about anything. She had a good position as a music teacher, but didn't really take care of us at all. There were never any clean clothes in the house and then she would yell at me when I took some of hers to go to school. My father had left behind a huge amount of pills. My brother and I began to take them all. He was a drug dealer at the age of eight. I remember his big pharmacy scale to weigh the hashish he sold. I got a job to clean the bar around the corner. They paid me well, because there was lots of cocaine around the kitchen and bar and I never told anyone.

I had to change schools a lot because I was argumentative with the teachers who taught music and religion. I would easily get very angry. I was insane. My brother and I had many terrible fights. I had nobody else to hurt, so I just hurt him. The last time he beat me up was when I was eight months pregnant.

At nineteen I traveled to India with a girlfriend. I used the money I had earned from a modeling job. We smoked some heroin on our first night in Bombay and it felt good. I didn't understand that I became addicted and didn't know how to avoid becoming pregnant. I was hiding everything, took a lot of cocaine, and had seven abortions. When I became pregnant with my daughter, everything was different. Her dad was my big love, although he lived in another country with his girlfriend, who also got pregnant at the same time and never found out about our daughter. It was more difficult than I thought to actually stop doing cocaine, but I knew I had to do it.

My baby was born on a very cold night before Christmas. My mother and brother had left. I was alone at the hospital. My girlfriend came the next day and we smoked a cigarette. Having a daughter changed everything. I tried to be the best mother in the world. I learned from my girlfriend how to treat my baby and did everything exactly how she said to do it. I'm so glad I did. It was hard without a job or a man, although I did get welfare for a year. Then I went back to school and eventually got stable work.

I began working a recovery program and have been sober since 11/1/2001. In years of therapy I realized that I had depression as a child, probably as a consequence of the neglect and abuse. Also, it used to confuse me when my mother would tell me that I only imagine these things. The truth is that my memories can be a bit blurry. Things can seem vague, and everything was always overwhelmingly shameful. I would still prefer that all of this weren't true, but my life is good now. I am very happy about my teenage daughter and that I was able to love and protect her. She is the best. She came into my life like an angel. I don't ever have to go back to my old life.

7. ...THE MORE I LOVE MY CATS

LIVED IN THE SAME HOUSE in Speedway, Indiana, for many years. It was haunted, or maybe I haunted it or the emptiness did. My parents had moved there so that my dad could be next to the racetrack—where he died in a car race when my mom was pregnant with me. I think I was stewing in her grief. I was born a blue baby.

My childhood was normal enough, given the circumstances. There was an empty feeling, a lifeless quality, surreal, like a Dali painting. Time had weight. There was love there, but I don't think I could count on it. It couldn't be grabbed. I used to walk to the church up the street as a phone booth to my dad. My mom was at work. There was TV and TV dinners. I had my sister for a while. We were best friends until she hit puberty and was off.

At eighteen I took my toolbox, my dog, and my plant in the Chevy van and left for California. A few years went by and I enlisted in the army. I still think of myself as a soldier. I was shipped to Texas, Hawaii, Korea, and a lot in Thailand and Malaysia. On my twenty-fifth birthday I had a bar fight that left me in a coma for ten days. After that, I couldn't talk for a long time until I slowly learned it again. I'm still dyslexic from that. I had just gotten married, which turned out not to be such a good idea.

I went to college in San Francisco on a scholarship and got a B.F.A. in painting. I loved college, I guess, because I was focused then. I have always thought of myself as a painter, although I drew more than I painted while I was in the army. But I had unreasonable rage after the head trauma and began a dangerous lifestyle. I had motorcycles and guns, and played Russian roulette. I used to be a bar drinker, and later a lone drinker. I needed alcohol to fall asleep.

I had to escape the loneliness of my life with women who were bad for me but still better than being without anyone. I had some relationships that didn't go well. In fact, I don't think any of them went well. I had trust issues. I was obsessive and jealous, and I had some compulsions. I wasn't violent with women, though. My first wife was a crazy and possessed Christian. The second one died of a heroin overdose while I was in treatment. The third one had HIV. I got arrested a lot with her. I remember smoking our last cigarette together, in Virginia, with handcuffs on. We were married and divorced, too, by an Indian shaman in Boulder, Colorado. I was very careful not to have a child. I didn't want to not be around like my dad.

Sometimes I get overwhelmed. I live in my head. Depression is a huge part of my life. I call it "the grip." It is a spiritual, emotional, and physical pain. Self-centered ego seems like mud to me. I don't want to deal with it and I don't like to deal with money and clients. I am shy—most of the time I would rather observe than engage.

On April 14, 2003, I had to get sober. I was done. Everything in my head broke. I felt sick and dead. Although I still get bent out of shape, I'm O.K. now and I know serenity. I don't like to be around people much, but I go to twelve-step meetings and I have done my twelve steps. I have a few friends and four cats. I really care about my cats. I take time to be present with them, to make them feel safe and loved. They are my closest example of a caring and loving God.

8. FLOWER CHILD

NEVER KNEW WHO I WAS. My entire life I'd been in total confusion. I didn't even know what shoes or movies I liked. I was unaware. It might have been because I had to shut off my emotions. I think I learned it when I was four and my mom would beat up my oldest sister. She remained scarred for life from my mom's nails. It was my dad, though, who threw her down the stairs (only once). My mom was mentally ill and my dad was weak. It was intense. My mother would forever close the windows so the neighbors wouldn't hear the screaming; my sister would open them so people could hear what was going on, and my mom would get even madder. This went on for many, many years. I was utterly confused because I loved them all, and I used to deny that these things ever happened. I remember nothing. I am so glad that I was able to tell my sister on her deathbed that in fact she was just a little child and these things were never her fault. She said then that she had been waiting all these years for me to admit that she had been the victim.

Right now, I'm feeling balanced. I have been out of balance, though, because of what I had to handle on the physical plane. I did use the spiritual tools I have learned in my recovery and they got me through. However, I had not processed the loss and grieving that came with my cancer diagnosis and treatment. I didn't realize it, because I had shut off my feelings. As a consequence, I couldn't feel compassion for anyone else either. It looks like I have hurt some people recently without even knowing it.

I want to talk about the drugs, though—not so much about the problems. My mother told me that I used to get a sore throat as a little girl and I always wanted the codeine cough medicine that she would give me, but I didn't drink or use much in high school. By then it was the late sixties and seventies and I became a hippie. I believe I was a product of the time. I went to love-ins, lived in a commune, and I took LSD, PCP, MDA, peyote, pot, everything. I stole pills from my mom, too. I'm glad for all the experiences I had. They were mind-expanding. I drank a lot, too. When I was twenty-seven, I began to snort heroin. But things didn't get really bad until I began to shoot up. From thirty to thirty-eight that's all I did, three times a day. In the winter, my ex and I would spend three months in South America doing cough medicine and pills.

In 1988 I was sick and tired of being sick and tired. I went to Provincetown and cold-turkey'd it for a week. I was sick as a dog. Then I started drinking alcohol for eight months and that's the only time I got pregnant and had an abortion. Drinking brought me to my knees. I heard then that this disease is cunning, baffling, and powerful and I saw that it was true.

The only thing I know about getting sober is that it's God's grace, but what kept me sober was rolling up my sleeves and getting to work with my sponsor and my therapist. I basically met myself. I allowed God in on a daily basis, which means that I live in acceptance. I want my spiritual connection to be the main part. If I thought that I could get high a couple of times a year, I would do it in a New York second, but I know that after picking up I wouldn't want to just get high once. If I pick up, the obsession will take over and I won't be able to stop. I love my life now and I wouldn't trade it.

9. THE NAÏVE BOUNCER

MY GRANDPARENTS HAD SURVIVED the Holocaust and moved to Israel, where they adopted my dad. My mom was an American nurse who had come to Israel at twenty-one years old to help out after a war. They moved to a kibbutz in a very small town. By the time I was born, they were already on a hate rampage. They got divorced before I had the chance to realize what life was all about. We stayed at the kibbutz with my dad when my mom moved back to the U.S., until one night she returned and kidnapped me and my brothers, in the middle of the night, and smuggled us to New York with fake passports. Nine months later, my dad won the ensuing custody battle and took us back to Israel. My problem as a kid was with God. If there is a loving God, then why was I dealt this mess? I loved booze from the moment it hit my lips when I was thirteen. I loved the Purim holiday, where people are supposed to get drunk. I was forever waiting for the next Purim to come around.

One day after I got released from the army (at twenty), I left for some R & R (rest and relaxation), Whisky, and pot in Thailand. I enjoyed my five-month vacation there, but my aspirations had always been to become an actor, so I went to live with my mom in California. Too naïve to notice what was going on, I took a job as a bartender in a gay bar. I was also the default bouncer there.

I loved throwing people out and it was all fun for a while, but I had to move on to Venice Beach and get my own apartment. The first six months at Venice were the highlight of my life so far. Everything was wonderful. Drinking like a fish and smoking pot, I wore a lot of colorful clothes, purple sunglasses, and bandanas to go with my orange suede bellbottom pants. I was totally living the sixties (it was around 1993).

But when I did cocaine, everything changed. Within a couple of months, I had an eviction notice. One morning the cops came. I had been up all night, waiting for them. I had my little backpack ready to go and I went straight to the dealer's house a block away. Then came the period that I choose to call "homelessness." I lived in bushes and under the lifeguard stand. It was just one lonely, bizarre, and disgusting situation after another, and it went down from there. I tried to control my using, but I couldn't. The night of the motorcycle accident was significant. The crash happened at exactly the same time my grandma passed away in Israel. I was more close to her than to anybody else. She was the only one who gave me that feeling of unconditional love. I took this strange coincidence as a sign to get me connected to God again, but still couldn't stop using.

I went off the deep end the night I got arrested for assault with a deadly weapon (a baseball bat) on six charges. Six people had to go to the hospital, two of them cops (just for the record,

I didn't hit all of them with the baseball bat). The truth is I just wanted to have a good time. I really didn't want to hurt anybody. They should have left me alone for a moment. I would have left me alone—but they tried to force me down. My pot must have been laced with some PCP, because I had this super strength during the fight. Luckily I had a hallucination of a peaceful and smiling Jesus when one of the cops was sitting on my head and I let go of my plan to snatch one of their guns and win the fight (I know how to handle guns really well). They beat me up very badly after that and I was in jail for six months.

I had a lot of voices in my head. I wanted to get sober after I got out of jail, but I didn't. What got my attention was hearing that I would enjoy peace of mind through recovery in a twelve-step program. When my girlfriend was taken to rehab in November 1995, I came back to L.A. on a Greyhound bus and began to go to meetings every day. I got a sponsor, did the steps, and began sponsoring people after a few months. Not drinking or using is just a part of it. The real recovery is that I can actually function in society and function with myself—that I am sane. I understand now that there is no good or bad—my life is perfect. Everything that happened was necessary for my spiritual evolution. I feel a connection with my Higher Power and I have a purpose—to learn, to teach, to experience, and to evolve as a spiritual being. That's my purpose in this lifetime. Everything else is just decoration.

10. KIRSTEN, ESCAPE ARTIST

GREW UP WITH LOVING PARENTS, an only child until I was ten and my brother was born. I spent a lot of time alone. It didn't help that my dad was an alcoholic and drank liquor out of his coffee mug every morning. My mom worked. I was taught that emotions were scary and when you feel them you should freak out and blow up. I thought that women's tears were black, because my mom had big black tears rolling down her face when she cried. I spent my days in a dream world with imaginary friends, drawings, and dolls. I knew that this world was bad to live in and I tried to escape through fantasy. My reality as a child was that life was lonely, chaotic, and scary. I was confused and just wanted to be loved, but instead felt forgotten about. Don't get me wrong—I did have love in my home, but it was marinated in alcoholism, which became my "normal." I couldn't just daydream when my grandmother fell off the kitchen counter, drunk, singing Patsy Cline songs in between screaming at me, or when my strung-out uncle kept stealing.

Growing up, I was constantly seeking escape. The forms changed as I got older and things stopped working. Then I found drugs and booze. I soon knew no other way of seeing the world.

I remember just hating myself and feeling like I never fit in. By thirteen, I had developed an eating disorder and had begun experimenting with drugs and alcohol. I was obsessed with my eating habits and soon was addicted to diet pills and cigarettes. I barely graduated college. My friends all went away. I had achieved what I always wanted as a little girl—to live in my own world. I remember calling myself an "escape artist" and took it on as a proud identity. After years of moving around every four months, starting over, just to find myself and this life again, I finally got tired and just allowed my disease to totally rule me. I knew that I drank more than other people, and this became very clear to me when I actually did drink at a bar. I was constantly humiliating myself because I could never just have one. I hated that. So I began to drink at home, alone. I hated everyone and was so scared to be around people. For two years before I got clean and sober, all I did was go to work, come home, and get drunk until I passed out. I didn't have contact with anyone outside of my work.

I found myself in recovery so completely randomly. My father had gotten sober when I was ten, so I knew it wasn't all bad. I had gotten my dad back. That must have been why, in a drunken hangover fog, after a particularly embarrassing night, I went to a twelve-step meeting. Looking back, it seems like some Higher Power got me there—getting sober had never been a conscious thought for me. I had not known there was another way to live. I saw people who looked like me and said the things that I thought, and I felt like I fit in, truly. It was a new experience. My most humiliating story could make my new friends laugh—because they had been there. I got a sponsor and began working the steps for recovery. Following her suggestions has kept me sober. I go to meetings every day and I try my best to do the next right action, to stay in the moment, to *allow* myself to stay in the moment. I can see that the way I tried to deal with my problems led me to a dark corner of the planet where I didn't want to live. So, my choice is to get sober and get a better experience with life.

11. VICTIMS R US

NEVER LIKED WHERE I WAS, and so I used to run away from home. One morning I left and walked around town all day. Eventually I panhandled some dinner. Around midnight I was walking along Pico Boulevard close to the Fox Studios in Los Angeles. I was really tired and thought I'd sleep in one of the sand traps at the golf course and catch a rabbit for breakfast in the morning. I was five years old. When a family friend who had found me drove me home, the lights were on, there were policemen, people everywhere, and women in curlers. I was baffled. When my mom saw me, she screamed. My sister slapped me (she always hated me). I was astonished that they had noticed I was gone. It never occurred to me that my behavior affected other people. This is probably my disease. It began to change when I got sober, but my fear remained that, any minute, I would be found out to be a fraud and I would be humiliated and shamed again. I felt like I was living behind enemy lines.

My dad had never wanted a boy child. He wanted to be the only boy in the house. He got sober when I was ten, but still had a bad temper. I was terrified of him. I stayed away from my family a lot. I was the outsider, always. We talked about safe and superficial things only, like the Dodgers, woodwork, fishing, boats, or airplanes. They got very upset if I ever came up with anything serious or emotional.

My dad had tried to kill me a couple of times in a drunken rage, but I had forgotten all of that. Many years into my recovery, at a meeting for adult children of alcoholics, it suddenly came back. I was a little guy, curled up in a fetal position, as my dad screamed: "Die, you little bastard!" As the images surfaced, I wailed and howled. I came unglued. I was ripped open and all this disgusting ugly stuff came out. Flooded with these memories, I was unspeakably angry. I understood that I needed recovery. I didn't want to run around my whole life blaming my father. I wanted healing, and I also didn't want it. It scared me. I had felt like a victim for so long. I remember consciously giving up my position of being a victim and letting go of my rage when I asked: "God, please let me see him through your eyes."

This is what happened and this was the great lesson for me. They had to call me (I didn't call). I drove down to see them. My dad and I were sitting together, watching a ball game. I observed myself being comfortable until my dad made a disparaging joke about me. I turned to him and said quietly, "Hey, Pop, I wish you wouldn't do that." He didn't get it and asked, "Do what?" So I told him that he had put me down in front of Mom. He went crazy. He turned purple yelling at me. I got up and went outside, but he still carried on. I understood then that he felt scared and inadequate just like me, that he protected himself with this rage. I couldn't take it personally anymore, because I knew the truth. This is what he did to cover his fear. When I finally went back in, he patted my knee and said, "Well, my old man used to do that." We both cried like little kids, until he finally said: "Now cut it out, damn it, you're making a dame out of me." We could talk then, because we were not afraid of each other anymore.

I have been sober since September 25, 1961, when I was twenty-six years old. My dad has been gone for a long time, and I'm learning again about detachment, I guess—how to not become involved in people's disaster when they make their victimhood their identity. There is no power in that, or delight. There is nothing in the victim role, really. I have compassion, but I don't support victimhood today in myself or in others. I hear the drama. Instead of comforting, I say, "Are you willing to have a healing occur?" Sometimes they defend their pain.

12. GLAMOUR RAPE

W HEN I WAS LITTLE, we moved a lot. I was always the "new kid."
We didn't just move towns. We moved countries—Egypt,
Yemen, Saudi Arabia, UAE, Greece, Spain, Malaysia, Thailand.
When I was nineteen years old I moved from Bangkok, Thailand,
to Los Angeles to go to USC. I had grown up in a lifestyle that
entailed private schools, maids, drivers, and vacations to Bali,
Tokyo, Micronesia, or Myanmar. I knew no one in L.A., and I liked
it that way.

I just wanted to be beautiful, loved, and removed—in a pal-
ace made of ice or on a yacht in the South of France sipping
champagne, doing lines of cocaine with some guy telling me
how hot I am (but I honestly don't think I have loved anyone,
ever). My parents would tell me that this was a bad idea and
that these things don't lead to happiness. But when I finally got
away from my parents, that's exactly what I decided to do.

My dad came out to L.A. for parents' weekend in the fall of
my freshman year and introduced me to one of his friends who
owned a very trendy restaurant in Beverly Hills. When we had
dinner with this friend, he gave me his number and told me to
call him if I ever needed anything. My dad told me to stay away
from him. So I called the guy and he invited me to come and
have free dinners at his restaurant whenever I liked and bring

my girlfriends. So I did. We would often go out to clubs in his limo with his little entourage. No standing in lines. No need for fake IDs. All the cocaine and top-shelf alcohol I could consume for free. He would give me spending money and I thought he liked me because I am funny and pretty. One night after hitting the clubs, we were at his house in Beverly Hills and we were alone upstairs in his bathroom, snorting line after line as the party raged on below us. Suddenly he hugged me and I hugged him back, not thinking much of it. I don't want to talk about the details, but he raped me. And afterward I did another line and went back downstairs to join my friends. I never said anything to anyone.

I kept sleeping with him after he had raped me. For the next six months every time I saw him we had sex. Keep in mind that this person was way more than twice my age and not remotely attractive. I started sleeping with other much older men and with his brother, too. Once, his brother almost shot me. I did things that should make me feel sick to my stomach to even think about, but I can talk or write about it as though it happened to someone else. It is like it happened to a different person because I wasn't there. Physically I was there, but mentally I was far away in fantasyland. Nothing really mattered.

I despised him and I felt like a slut. So I guess I began to despise myself, too. I didn't want anybody to know about what

I was doing. I pretended to study at USC for two and a half years after I had dropped out. My parents eventually cut me off financially and I had to go to rehab for six months, but I still couldn't see the point in any of this, really. I am being told that I am still indifferent to myself or disconnected from my truth or something like that. I don't really know. I feel a little sad from time to time, but I am only twenty-four years old and have been clean and sober for three months. I have a sponsor, I go to meetings, and I am staying away from men totally. I share a loft in downtown L.A. with two other women, and I work long hours. I am trying something different now—delaying gratifications and following suggestions. I think I have been stupid and feel ashamed about it, but sometimes it seems like my old life was more glamorous.

13. LIVE COMBAT

MY HOME WAS THE MOST UNSAFE PLACE on the planet for me. I didn't realize that until later. I was abused emotionally and physically. My dad was a WWII combat Marine veteran. I think he never really came away from the war and he took us all hostage. I carried that into adult life. He was a blackout drinker and he would cry. I still hear his voice of abuse every night. He was who he was. My mother fit into the role of what somebody like my father needed. They stayed together until she died.

There is no doubt in my mind that I am genetically predisposed to be an alcoholic. My sister, who was five years older than me, led me in that direction, because she was already there when I was eight. I was angry, disruptive, and inconsistent, but the drinking didn't really start until I was about eleven. It progressed from there. The drugs were rapidly following suit. I was using intravenous drugs when I was fifteen. Academically I tested in the 99th percentile nationally (in math) and attended all the advanced classes up until tenth grade when my sister died and I dropped out. There was only anxiety, fear, and rage (which I used to protect myself). I don't remember much and I didn't show up at her funeral. I understand now that we had a so-called "trauma bond" and were connected with special intensity and this is why her abandonment was so absolutely devastating to me.

I didn't have the stamina to keep going without getting sick all the time, because I have hepatitis C. It was not working and so I got sober when I was twenty-four, which was twenty-five years ago. I saw that I could either become a professional criminal or join the human race. I called AA. Someone came to take me to a meeting. I had a spiritual experience that day. I looked at the sky and the stars and felt this tremendous relief, like a weight had been lifted. I was crying a lot that day, which was unusual for me. I feel like I am a citizen of the universe, just a piece of something much larger than me.

For thirty-eight years I never knew what was wrong with me. I was not conscious of my feelings at all. I did not know love from sadness or pity from compassion. I had not cried for seven years when I went down to the beach one Christmas Day and melted. That's when I was finally able to begin the process of mourning the loss of my sister. I have been in intense therapy for my PTSD, which I had never identified until my father died. Eventually I was able to find a sharp decline in my trigger response. I look at my therapy journey like a dartboard. I think that my father had transferred to me the unspeakable horror he had gone through in live combat and I had been on high alert my whole life. I always knew that when he died I would be set free. I had been stuck behind a wall of hostility. When he was gone, a door opened and I was released.

The energy that had been passed on to me, I had to dispel it somehow. I wanted to broaden myself into a wider spectrum beyond anxiety, fear, and anger. I'm still on the path of healing. I live my sobriety and my life through the tools I have learned. This gives me a moment—where I have the choice to act in love. I can reach for connection in love and faith rather than disconnecting in fear and anger.

PART SIX

UNDERSTANDING
RECOVERY

Beginning anew is not easy.
We have to transform our hearts and our minds in very practical ways.
We may feel ashamed, but shame is not enough to change our heart. . . .
Beginning anew is not to ask for forgiveness.
Beginning anew is to change your mind and heart,
to transform the ignorance that brought about wrong actions of body,
speech, and mind, and to help you cultivate your mind of love.
Your shame and guilt will disappear,
and you will begin to experience the joy of being alive.
All wrongdoings arise in the mind.
It is through the mind that wrongdoings can disappear.

—from *Teachings on Love,* Thich Nhat Hanh

You, Me, My Cats, and Stephen Hawking

*There was a disturbance in my heart, a voice that spoke there
and said, I want, I want, I want!
It happened every afternoon, and when I tried to suppress it,
it got even stronger.
It only said one thing, I want, I want!*

—Saul Bellow

WHEN MY SON WAS BORN, I adored him and I loved him unconditionally. That's what mothers do. Babies are helpless
and need this kind of nurturing so they won't die. Those of us
who did not receive sufficient love and care in early childhood
tend to feel unlovable and "unworthy," remaining with perennial desires that cannot be fulfilled by outside sources once the
window has closed.

The experience of one's neediness and the inability to satisfy it ("I can't get no satisfaction") gets translated into greed and gluttony and, on the basis of predisposing genetics, into an addictive personality. Addicts keep on searching for someone who will love them unconditionally. They feel that they have nothing to give and thus find it impossible to establish satisfying ways of relating. Instead, they hide their shame about feeling unlovable by withdrawing and getting loaded. In the process, they reinforce their self-image of not being "worthy"—by neglecting to engage in activities they would feel good about while pursuing a way of life they do not feel good about, which brings more shame and guilt. Addicts eventually feel useless, worthless, and hopeless, which they reinforce with more self-loathing and self-hatred, creating an even more desperate need to forget it all. The inability to love oneself turns into self-hatred, expressed and communicated through a chain of destructive and self-defeating behaviors. This, then, is the self-destructive feedback loop in which addicts find themselves stuck.

Late-stage alcoholics usually don't live in mutually nurturing mature relationships, which are characterized by a balanced style of give and take. Their life is lonely and empty. Even if they still have some "loved ones" and some money, nothing is "working for them"; there is no happiness to be had. Addiction is not about having fun. It is about forgetting about oneself and the world and all the disappointments that came along with the experience of living.

A successful life is not about receiving unconditional love, though; nor is it about loving others unconditionally (which is the co-dependency illusion). It is about doing something useful on a daily basis, and using one's mind to create something that makes life worthwhile. You don't have to be a genius like Stephen Hawking to overcome adversity so that you can use your God-given talents. It's not all that hard. My cats do it every day. They live in the moment and do what they can. They cannot catch all the opossum babies they prey on, and they don't care whether I like it when they do. They do their thing.

THE PROMISES

" AM SO MAD AT HIM. He is stupid and mean. He has done me wrong. It's all his fault. I hate him. I will make him understand that he has to change." Jill sees her problem as being outside of her, where she has no control. As long as she thinks this way, she creates a toxic emotional environment for herself. She'll do what she has always done. She needs to drink or fight, eat, have sex, or something—something to dull her pain. Once she can own her problem, she can do something about it and won't have to seek oblivion from her misery.

There was a time when alcohol let her feel O.K. That time is gone. She can't find relief. Her life is in shambles now. She is sick and tired of being sick and tired. She can't stand being dysfunctional anymore. She wants to get sober, but the chaos she has created—the trail of her own wreckage—terrifies her to death. She is tortured with regrets and self-loathing. Where are her friends? She reads: *"An alcoholic is like a tornado roaring his way through the lives of others."* (Alcoholics Anonymous, page 82)

If only she could feel calm and confident! She doesn't know how to feel strong and capable. She carries her past injuries like trophies, "Look at what they have done to me." She has been avoiding dealing with things, so the world seems threatening. She always expects something from people, so she keeps on getting disappointed. As long as she insists on blaming others, she'll feel helpless and resentful. Her resentments are a spiritual malady. Can she see that she has a disease of perception, that she is her own victim? No one can tell her that she is not O.K.

If she wants to be sober, she must find a way to feel comfortable in her own skin. There are things she can do so the insanity of alcohol won't return. She can learn a new way of looking at things and have a psychic change. She can learn to walk through her fear and refuse to be intimidated by her own despair. She could be shown how to forgive herself and have a good life. All she has to do is be willing. What does she have to lose?

The twelve-step program of Alcoholics Anonymous promises that we get a chance to comprehend serenity and know peace—"a new freedom and a new happiness." Sounds sweet when you're coming from hell, doesn't it? Through working the steps, a metamorphosis is initiated from a being that causes pain through the relentless pursuit of selfish pleasure, to a different kind of being who uses his or her experiences and gifts to benefit others. This may not sound like much, but it makes all the difference. The only way to know this transformation is by going through it. Imagine the energy flow to be reversed during this process from being like a vacuum cleaner (forever sucking up everything into its emptiness and ends up full of garbage) to a spotlight that shines its light onto whatever is before it. The result of shining your love onto the creation you behold is a life in the light.

PSYCHOTHERAPY

ALCOHOLICS ANONYMOUS addresses the disease of alcoholism and outlines the most successful approach to recovery. Some alcoholics achieve sobriety and begin a new life as they follow the suggested twelve-step program. So far, so good. If your primary issue or addiction is not addressed in your recovery plan—if you experience depression, consistent anxiety, PTSD, or other overwhelming emotional states or intrusive thought processes, if you have an anger problem or difficulties with relationships, you may find it impossible to maintain your sobriety with AA alone.

Many of us grew up in dysfunctional families without sufficient support, guidance, and encouragement. Some of us have been subjected to abuse, violence, and/or incest, having had to find some kind of way to survive emotional pain. You may have been emotionally neglected during a difficult childhood without much tender love and care. Early recovery can be stressful if you become overwhelmed with feelings you don't understand. When old memories surface at this time, it can be of great importance to be able to feel safe with an experienced professional. It can make all the difference to see a psychotherapist in order to work through some of your painful childhood experiences—so that you have a real chance to deal with your personal issues after all this time of trying to forget. This might be what it takes to stay sober and get a good life.

FOOD FOR THOUGHT

IT HAS BEEN SAID that an alcoholic alone is in bad company, which is why alcoholics try to distract themselves from themselves by hanging out in bars, making lengthy long-distance phone calls during the night, and having sex with strangers, as long as they can… Chances are, when you get sober your thinking process will be morbid (mine was), incessantly producing scary and depressing contents. You may think that these are thoughts—and they have been called "automatic thoughts"—but in fact they are remembered thoughts, the oldies of a person stuck in a repetition compulsion—the same theme song plays over and over, with the same results. They say, if nothing changes, nothing changes. In the absence of some good heroin (or whatever you preferred), it's time to feed your recovering brain with some new ideas. If you go to one AA meeting a day in your early recovery, you get a break from your obsessions and hear something else instead. If you hear things you don't like, don't dispute them—simply discard them. Don't waste your (limited) energy on controversy. Many bloody wars have been fought over "God's wishes." The truth is, nobody knows for sure.

In addition, I strongly recommend that you get the big Alcoholics Anonymous book. Remember and learn whatever you find helpful and interesting. Look at it as a buffet—listen, read, and choose what resonates within you. If you are confused, that's something to talk, write, or pray about. Other spiritual books have been instrumental in my own recovery, as well. After having relied on chemical substances, my brain had been malnourished for too long to produce anything pleasant—I had to feed it some new things. This is where a sponsor comes in. Without any new content in your brain, you WILL fall back on whatever it is that you have learned so far—the "comfort zone" of your familiar but self-destructive habits. A sponsor can teach you how they stayed sober. Be willing to try some new thoughts and behaviors. What have you got to lose?

PERCEPTION

PERCEPTION IS A CREATIVE ACT OF computing reality in order to give meaning to objects, events, and circumstances. Our perceptions are based considerably on childhood experiences, less on later life events, and even less on present reality. Events need to be analyzed so that we can decide whether they are important or irrelevant; some are familiar and we assume that we know what they mean. We tend to disregard information that conflicts with our preexisting beliefs. This process of "selective inattention" saves us from sensory overload and enables us to react swiftly. This means that perception is cumulative. We determine our present "reality" based on previous perception.

We assume that things will continue to happen as they have in the past. We expect new acquaintances to behave just like the people we already know. Grown up in a safe and nurturing environment, we tend to trust the future. Grown up with emotional or physical abuse, we may maintain "learned helplessness," where we assume that we cannot do much to improve a bad situation. This reliance on past experience is originally an adaptive response. It simplifies life, as it saves us from having to analyze each experience. However, we may draw erroneous conclusions. After all, circumstances do change. This necessitates some discernment, reevaluation, adaptation, and adjustment so that we may grow with our tasks and mature as we adopt some new coping mechanisms from time to time.

As long as we live in our disease, we avoid and reject reality for what it is. We seek illusion and oblivion. We refuse to engage, participate, and take responsibility. So we deny ourselves the opportunity to correct faulty assumptions and to heal. We are not really present to explore our painful memories, grieve our losses, deal with our issues, and move on.

Instead of addressing our emotional wounds and mastering today's challenges, we get stuck in a past world, eternally wounded and victimized. While we maintain our own dysfunctional attitudes and behaviors, we self-righteously criticize and blame others who appear on our path, blind to the misery we cause for all. Without recovery we may end up in a repetition compulsion just like in the movie *Groundhog Day*, where the same day must be relived over and over.

The past is long gone. Even though we may have been wounded, we are not the helpless victims we once were. We have grown. We can embrace the power we have today. We can assert ourselves. We can liberate ourselves from painful memories. Even though some people are not trustworthy, we can find people to trust. While difficulties may arise, peace and beauty exist, as well. It is important to discern what's going on right here right now without catastrophic assumptions and generalized resistance. Instead of complaining about the past, we can seize the present and commit to recovery. We can decide not to do unto others what has been done unto us. A successful life is an active life, lived in the present with the intention of bringing to the day what we like to have.

WOUNDS

SOME OF US HAVE SURVIVED abuse, abandonment, violence, or incest. We were injured when we needed to be nurtured. We were made to feel worthless when we could have used some self-esteem, discouraged when we needed hope. We were victimized when we should have been protected. Like Michael Jackson, we may feel like children forever when the world knows that we are adults. We suffer from countless fears and insecurities. Some of us cover up with anger. Some of us project our angry impulses onto others and self-righteously resent them for it, so we can keep the self-image of an innocent victim. Oblivious to the effect we have on others, we have excuses for all our irresponsible and destructive behaviors. We may over-identify with our wounds as if that's all we are—"Look what they have done to me." Friends may leave us, spouses may divorce us, employers may let us go, and we blame the world as we refuse to look at our own conduct. It's not all that much fun to deal with us…

Most of us found substances early on to feel powerful, confident, invincible, and to dull the pain. They worked for a while and then they caused more disaster than they let us forget. At first we were glad to find some self-medication. We didn't see it as the problem. It was our solution. Our toxic brain hasn't matured in a normal manner, and our emotional growth has been stunted. As we sought oblivion, we didn't attend to our wounds, and they haven't healed. Waking up in recovery, we find that they are festering and hurting—our resentments have been keeping us in pain. Forgiving does not mean that we find excuses or minimize what has been done. It is about realizing that it's over, that we can find peace only through forgiveness. We have the chance to be aware and move on. The prison gates are open—all we have to do is walk through. We are free to forgive and heal.

RED-LIGHT DISTRICT

PSYCHOLOGISTS UNDERSTAND that our character and belief system is formed in childhood, mostly within the first six to twelve months of life, based on our experiences during that time. For example, "Life is good" (I am getting what I need as soon as I need it); "I am powerful" (when I cry, my mom comes and takes care of me); "Pain is all there is" (no matter how much I cry, nobody cares). Unless they are corrected, these core beliefs usually persist throughout adult life.

As children we experience consequences of our own actions, observe the behaviors of others, seek to understand our role in life, and begin to put together our beliefs. Around the age of eight, some of us form a "life script" based on relevant life circumstances. For example, "I am lovable the way I am" (I am being loved unconditionally); "I hate men" (I am a victim of abuse and/or incest); "I am bad/ugly/stupid" (I have been shamed, disrespected, and discouraged).

Red lighting has been used in "red-light districts" to make things look different and create an ambiance for certain experiences. Imagine for a moment that your favorite color is blue and your least favorite color is purple. Now imagine that a long time ago you installed a red filter on the lens of your mental eye and have forgotten that it's there. The result would be that all things blue look purple to you. Even the sky looks purple. You can't find your favorite color no matter where you look, even though it's there. The tinted filter changes everything.

Core beliefs and life scripts can work like a filter that distorts your perceptions. As a consequence, you experience the world in a different light. You may search tirelessly for something that's right in front of you, and not see it. You may become discouraged and give up, possibly turning to addictions to forget your hopelessness. In recovery we get the chance to change the filter of early programming and correct faulty perceptions. It is an important aspect of the work that must be done. Some of us need psychotherapy to let emotional wounds heal and to release negative beliefs.

Remind yourself that your childhood pain is not happening today. If you haven't been happy lately, check your filter, and do whatever it takes to become whole and free so that you may shine your light on this day.

The mind is its own place and in itself,
can make Heaven of Hell, and a Hell of Heaven.

—John Milton

PSYCHIC CHANGE

Mental health is dedication to reality at all costs...

—M. Scott Peck

As ADDICTS, WE ARE MOST COMMITTED to escaping reality. We chase after delusions and so we attach our power to substances, which induce perceptual changes and help us to disconnect from reality. We obstinately carry on until our internal euphoria supply is exhausted and we are left empty and desperate. In recovery we are meant to withdraw our spirit from the insatiable object of desire. In order to accomplish this, we must be willing to undergo a psychic change and find a way to befriend reality. We are offered spiritual principles as tools for this essential psychological reorientation. A gradual shift in our thought process alters our perception and transforms our reality as a friendlier emotional climate emerges. While faith replaces fear, obsessive cravings wither away and we get the chance to experience life in a novel, more hopeful way. As a consequence, we are empowered to set in motion more functional behavior patterns and turn our fate around.

In recovery we let go of judgmental attitudes and take responsibility for our own actions and our well-being. We take our power back from excessive attachments and expectations.

We learn how to let go of resistance and defiance, replace it with acceptance, and become willing to seek out more functional behaviors. People begin to react differently to us, as well. Gradually a different reality begins to emerge. We are creatures of habit, though. We like to keep the momentum going and stick with the familiar, even if it's not working for us. The unknown can be scary. This is why "hitting bottom," where we cannot stand our misery anymore, is considered important. This so-called "gift of desperation" can compel us to surrender and be willing to learn a new way of life.

In the basic text of Alcoholics Anonymous, Dr. Bill Silkworth states that the chronic alcoholic must experience "an entire psychic change" (AA, pg. xxvii). He proposes a solution to overcome this otherwise hopeless condition via "twelve steps" to recovery. The program uses a spiritual orientation and concepts of cognitive-behavioral therapy to encourage and support a psychic change.

We are guided to surrender to a Higher Power and adopt moral principles. In order to let go of toxic attachments and resentments, it is suggested that we take a good look at our own actions only. We see that self-obsessed fear, self-indulgence, and indecent behaviors bring about suffering. We are shown how to give meaning to our shameful memories—by sharing our experiences so they can benefit others. Self-esteem is restored through making amends for the past, and doing estimable acts in the present. We find the strength to endure unpleasant feelings and difficult life phases. As we live recovery one day at a time, we replace fear and resentments with serenity and peace. We focus on kind and responsible behavior at all times. We turn from our own worst enemy into our own best friend.

This is our chance to recover our life's purpose and become useful family members, good friends, and respectable people. It is the path of liberation from the slavery of compulsive need gratification at any cost. It may seem like a paradox, but this is what happens: we admit our powerlessness and regain our power of choice.

MOMENTUM

A s I SAID, WE ARE CREATURES OF HABIT. We are able to function because we have learned to do things habitually, so that we may attend to the moment and learn new things. Our habits have momentum, which essentially means that we feel like continuing to do what we are doing, while change requires some effort.

Imagine riding on a train. The train and the environment have been provided by a Higher Power, but you are the conductor of your train. Think about where you want to go. Whether you are going fast or slow, you will end up where the track takes you. Make sure you know your destination, so you won't go in the wrong direction. If the landscape has changed and you don't like it anymore, you might want to consider going to a different place. Make your decision—if you want to change where you are going, you must step on the brakes. It may take some effort to slow down until you come to a full stop, then change the switch and accelerate again. It will take some time to gain speed and momentum, but you'll be happy to be heading in the direction of where you want to be.

Choosing recovery is a little like that. Even though you are used to doing things in a certain way, you can change. Please don't ever forget that what you do today is up to you. Your life started out in a certain emotional, social, and financial climate. Take a good look around. Do you like where you are? If you don't, you are free to check out a new way of life, although the switch from your old way of life to the new one does require some courage, time, and commitment to the task at hand. Finding the right path may take some deliberation, work, and help from others. You might find it humiliating to admit that you have been going the wrong way for a long time. However, without change, you can't find the right way.

URGENT IMPULSES

RECENT SCIENTIFIC RESEARCH DEMONSTRATES that our brain activity does not differentiate between fact and fiction, reality and imagination. The brain shows the same activity whether you imagine a lemon, for example, or see it physically before you. We are also endowed with the ability to be aware of thinking about the lemon and to direct our thinking away from this image, if we so desire. This is our power. We can use it any way we like—beneficially or destructively. If we don't want to stimulate the response of salivating, it's a good idea not to imagine a lemon.

These findings have important implications for newly recovering addicts, who are confused and struggling with cravings. Don't indulge in pleasant memories of the early days when using drugs was sweet and painless! This so-called "euphoric recall" can initiate irresistible urges that trigger a relapse. You may also be troubled by extreme desires for a variety of comforting distractions. The lust for sex, love, or food can interfere with the chance for recovery when you make it a priority and feed it with today's life power. If you allow sad, hopeless, or angry feelings to persist, you will counteract your motivation to stay sober. Some people think they must fulfill their responsibilities to their family or career immediately. This can camouflage an unwillingness to master the challenge of early recovery, and they can end up overwhelmed, relapse, and never fulfill these same obligations. Put your recovery first! Everything else must wait. The time for it will come.

In early sobriety, while your brain is reestablishing its own natural biochemical functioning, you are vulnerable to excessive anxiety, anger, or sexual urges, which arise during this transitional phase. It is necessary to self-regulate this emotional dysregulation, which tends to be uncomfortable, especially if it persists for an extended period of time. Otherwise, you might be tempted to act out (self-)destructively. Don't give up on recovery just yet!

Your urgency and despair don't necessarily mean anything, except that your brain is adjusting. Chances are, you are imagining or remembering something. Your irritation does not mean that anything is wrong at all. In order to stay afloat on the white waters of early sobriety, it helps to keep your attention on your safety, stability, and a structured daily routine.

This is the time for learning how to manage yourself. You learn not to act out blindly on impulses and momentary emotional urges. Understand that you must not indulge in the questionable luxury of pursuing thoughts and fantasies that should not be implemented. Explore new behaviors rather than mindlessly repeating dysfunctional old habits. Instead of acting impulsively, make it your new habit to deliberate before taking an action. Feed your mind with some spiritual literature on a daily basis. Support your emotional regulation. Relaxation is key. Keep extraneous interference and over-stimulating excitement to a minimum. Take regular walks in the park or at the beach, where you breathe deeply, listen to the wind, and watch some birds. Let the sun shine on you. Pray. Breathe. Put your attention on the present moment. Do whatever it takes to create and maintain an emotional balance. Your discomfort will pass. You know you can make it through hard times, because you have done so in the past. Use your power for your own good. Everybody recovers, unless they change their mind.

RADIO DAYS

- When you have anxiety—it is because you think scary thoughts.

- When you have persistent anxiety—the same scary thoughts, like oldies on the radio, are playing over and over in your mind.

- When you are angry—you haven't been getting what you wanted, and you have been thinking that you are right and the other person is wrong.

- When you have low self-esteem—you have been repeating to yourself that you are worthless, bad, ugly, stupid, and/or wrong—thinking you "should" be different.

- When you feel depressed—you are remembering having been hurt in the past, while being mean to yourself in the present.

- When you feel hopeless—you are thinking that things won't ever get better.

- When you feel lonely—you think that no one loves you and no one ever will.

As I mentioned, these habitual thought patterns have been called "automatic thoughts," but they are not so much thoughts as they are verbal memories that are being played repetitively in the mind. They bring to life and repeat remembered experiences while directing feelings and attitudes on an ongoing basis. This is how previous learning influences present behavior. Our mental activity never stops as long as our brain is alive, just like a radio that cannot be switched off. And just like music, this mental activity triggers feelings. What you can do, however, if you don't like what you're hearing, is change the channel. You don't have to spend the rest of your life listening to "Death Metal" if you don't want to. Initially you may not know how to stop the destructive remembered thoughts you keep repeating to yourself. One way out is to make a conscious decision to try new actions, where you create new thought contents.

Repeating positive affirmations can be a useful tool. For example, you could tell yourself: "I am exactly where I am supposed to be" or "I am allowed to be happy today" (see also "Positive Affirmations" and "It Is What It Is"). In a gradual process, negative beliefs can be replaced with new and more useful ones. Remember, learning something radically new (such as giving yourself permission to be happy) does require repetition.

You can raise your awareness and differentiate more clearly between thoughts, feelings, beliefs, and attitudes. Begin writing regularly in a journal, where you record your feelings and some of the thoughts that go along with them (instead of acting them out impulsively). For example, let's say you are feeling irritated or angry. You could put down: "annoyed with person x." Then write down what it is that x did (or didn't do). Add what you did (or didn't do). You will find that this process enables you to identify and examine the thoughts behind your feelings. Don't, for the time being, fight your current feeling state, even if it is unpleasant. Accept it. It is your truth—for now. You will develop understanding and gain power to restrain impulsive urges.

As alcoholics we seek relief from our own distorted perceptions, where we assume threats and become fearful because of previous experiences. Twelve-step work (especially Step Four) proposes a "thorough and fearless moral inventory" in order to take a look at our part in the development of our difficulties. Look for these telltale signs that your thinking might need some adjusting: defiance, laziness, procrastination, judgments, expectations, resentments, or a desire for oblivion. These attitudes express resistance against the truth. They can turn into stumbling blocks on the path of recovery.

Self-examination, particularly during the process of psychotherapy, unravels the "knots" in our thinking process. Unpleasant thoughts, which have been racing repeatedly through our minds, eventually slow down and become manageable. It is as though the volume of the internal radio is being turned down and the sound of past pain fades out while we become receptive for new channels. Recovery is a lot about understanding that we may have been wrong and reaching for the opportunity to alter habitual thought patterns. As a result we begin to feel hopeful, to try out more functional behaviors, and "magically" our life begins to turn around.

ANGER & AGGRESSION

I am sad when I'm mad at you, Mama.

—My son, Jesse, at age four

ANGER IS A FEELING, while aggression is a behavior and communicates what is going on inside of you. Aggression doesn't happen in a vacuum. It is related to your overall emotional climate such as fear and sadness. When you are happy, you are not angry. When you are angry, you are not happy.

If you act on your aggressive impulse, you cause harm to your own being before you even hurt the other person. You will find that certain thoughts and feelings are behind aggression, fueling it. Let's take a look at some of the thoughts. Anger is always self-righteous—you think that you are right and the other person is wrong. You think that they don't understand. You are not getting what you want. When your perception of yourself in your world is not satisfactory and you don't know how to change it, you may feel like acting out aggressively to whoever is before you. It may even be a stranger in traffic. The relief of lashing out is only very brief—anger feeds on itself and nothing gets resolved. Your behavior is the response to some unpleasant emotional state, which you try to get rid of. Instead, your anger creates more problems and more misery.

You may feel victimized and/or hopeless and overwhelmed with the life you created. You may feel powerless about finding something that works for you, ready to throw a temper tantrum and destroy something. Remember, anger is your own internal state. As such, it has nothing to do with reality. It does, however, create reality—as you are blaming or victimizing others, you create pain, and they will respond to your aggression. Your self-righteous attitude may not be helpful to anybody, including yourself. Acting out in anger tends to be stupid and destructive. Instead, how about looking at what's behind your anger?

I have found it most useful to consciously experience my anger as a physical sensation in my body (like pain), and to accept that it's there for the time being (like pain). Sit down, put your hands in your lap, and take a moment to breathe. Take paper and pen, and write down what you are thinking and feeling. You do not have to take the detour of destructive acting-out and subsequent self-loathing to look at your part in the problem and to find a solution to it. If you are an alcoholic in early recovery, most of your "good ideas" are not so good after all. Even if you find a solution that seems great, do not take action just yet! Give it some time. Chances are it's not such a good idea. Most probably the best course of action at this point is not to do anything. Quit expecting things from others. Use "minimal effort" and stop trying to force things to be what they are not! You will notice that your anger will dissipate after a little while, just like a deflating balloon. Only then will you be able to think clearly again. You'll be glad that you didn't act on it and you'll realize that it's not even a big deal. In recovery we learn to pause and think before we act, and we turn from impulsive old children into reasonable and confident adults.

Buddha likened anger to picking up a burning ember
in your bare hands with the intention of throwing it at another...

—Stephen Levine

RESENTMENTS

Two monks (most probably dressed in orange garb) went for a walking tour to a remote monastery. Approaching a mountain creek they saw a lovely young woman in pretty clothes trying to get across with her bags. Gallantly, the older monk lifted her up and carried her and her bags over to the other side. She thanked him graciously and they went their separate ways.

Upon arrival at the monastery, the young monk turned to the old monk with a serious look and said, "I couldn't forget what happened yesterday. I have been thinking all along that you shouldn't have made physical contact with a female. It's forbidden." The old monk replied with a gentle smile, "I left her there yesterday. Are you still carrying her?"

—Buddhist story

TRULY WISHED that things could be different. The others had made mistakes and I didn't like it. I did feel guilty about things I should have done and things I shouldn't have done, but I surely preferred not to be reminded. On the other hand, I held on to resentments and told the others repeatedly about their faults. Unlike the wise old monk, we reacted defensively and engaged in ongoing strife. It ruined everybody's mood, too.

When we are incapable of showing up for life in such a way that it pleases us, things don't get done the way we want them to. Frustrated and dissatisfied with ourselves, we dwell on blame. A judgmental attitude can mask ignorance, confusion, insecurity, conflict, jealousy, or envy, and as such it is revealing about the person who is holding a grudge. Like the young monk in the story, we may be unsure and confused about the right course of action. Sometimes we think we have been treated poorly and unfairly. Identifying with the victim role, we cry out for justice and vengeance, seeking allies for our cause. When we feel insecure about ourselves, we may at times feel the need to give in to jealous obsessions. We may secretly envy others for having a lucky fate. Seething with resentments, we are thinking, "It's all about me," and when we have problems, "It's all because of you." Stuck in futile involvement with a past that is long gone, we miss the opportunity to "seize the day" and claim the power we do have today. Engulfed by sadness, we may end up seeking oblivion from a hostile world.

Resentments and judgments, guilt, shame, and self-loathing are a "package deal." As long as we don't feel good about ourselves, we seek to criticize others in an attempt to feel better inside. Though we may be wrong, we blame without doubt. We befriend "lower companions" so that we can say that, in comparison, we are less sick. We convince ourselves that things were not as they should have been and people didn't behave the way they should have. Unfortunately, a judgmental attitude is not a successful strategy for self-worth and self-acceptance. Over time self-righteous indignation tends to rigidify, especially when we justify our own actions as responses to prior transgressions. Things can get confusing. This is not a recipe for truth-finding. As long as we remain resentful, we carry the burden of unfinished issues from the past. And as eager participants in an unhappy chain reaction, where nothing gets resolved, we become a burden to everyone. Even though people's actions may be questionable, a critical attitude continually induces more bitterness. Eventually people withdraw from us and we become lonely.

Throughout history, confession has been considered a valuable tool for emotional well-being. A detailed examination of our own thought and behavior patterns is also a major component of twelve-step work, because it is understood that shame (about who we are) and guilt (about what we have done) can cause intense discomfort and trigger a relapse. The way out is provided by taking an honest look at ourselves, where we confess our motivations and actions in order to liberate ourselves from the need to judge and blame. It is suggested to take outward action and make amends, too. As a result, we let go of ruminations about past predicaments. We find solutions and move on.

When we raise our awareness of ourselves and the consequences of our behavior, we find that we don't have to remain victims. In the process, we adjust our perceptions of others as well. When we pull our spirit (our life energy) back from the need to prove other people's faults (even if they *are* at fault) we begin to see that we have options. We cease to endow others with the responsibility for our situation. We implement change and engage in the process of healing and growing. We begin to live our truth. We replace resentments with understanding and compassion. Forgiving ourselves enables us to forgive them. It is only when we love ourselves that we bring forth a loving attitude. Only then can we own our power and have a good life.

Some of us were victimized in childhood, through no fault of our own. In this case, it is necessary to clarify that no such violation was ever deserved, no matter what the circumstances were. Childhood trauma can be difficult to overcome and may require psychotherapy, because in this case a person's identity is formed without the confidence that comes from being loved in a safe environment. It can be most helpful if the associated shame, confusion, and insecurity is worked through with the assistance of an experienced professional. Even in such cases, resentments mean that people are holding on to old pain, sometimes without their awareness. Victims often refuse to let go because they don't want to betray their "inner child" who was wounded long ago. It may take some time to grieve one's lost childhood and gain self-love with the understanding that those times are over for good. It is important to understand that maintaining resentments means holding on to suffering. It stands in the way of healing old wounds and finally becoming free of the past.

FORGIVENESS

They say there is no difference
between a teacher, friend, or foe.
I guess that means
that I could learn the lesson you brought along,
that I don't have to continue to spend all my time
justifying that I was right and you were wrong,
that I have reason to be grateful
for you coming into my life.

I was resentful toward you for doing what you do
and not fulfilling all my needs all the time.
I don't have to keep ruining my mood (and yours) by blaming you
and thinking about the punishment I think you deserve.
I forgive you for everything you did and didn't do
because I want to be free of the bondage of resentment
and move on to something better.
Please allow me to make amends to you
for hurting you with my self-righteous victim attitude
while I was busy being selfish and useless.

I am doing so much better when I take care of myself
and focus on giving to others what I thought I ought to get.

I don't want to destroy my life (and yours) anymore.
I realize now that we both could use some compassion
and have some fun in the short time we have left.

THE MOST IMPORTANT THING

RESENTMENT CAN BE a major stumbling block on the road to recovery, and relinquishing the need to place blame on others can be a truly liberating experience. This is just one side of the story, though. Even without knowing you, I can safely assume that you have hurt others as well as yourself, that you haven't lived up to your potential, and that you have been angry, unfair, envious, greedy, gluttonous, arrogant, lazy, and "lustful." All of this is part of being human. You may feel ashamed and try to hide some of your experiences, actions, and memories from others and even from yourself. If you do that, you will present a "false self" and your life may appear futile.

The awareness of our wrongdoings can give rise to guilt and shame, and can motivate us to amend our life. As long as we feel guilty, it may seem like we don't deserve happiness. Self-loathing essentially means that we get stuck in self-hatred and self-punishment, where we turn our aggression inward. This is futile and painful—we miss compassion for our own suffering and lack the necessary hope for carrying on. Continuous self-loathing can become toxic and compel us to sabotage our well-being, while denying that we are doing it. This is why it can take people right back to relapse. Addicts tend to treat themselves and others in an abusive manner and may justify their unkind behaviors with past errors, mistakes, and flaws.

You may over-identify with your past, thinking that what you have done until now is all that you are. You may feel like you are stupid, small, and/or broken—somehow not good enough. But I am telling you: You are a Divine child of God. You are beautiful, whole, and complete—just like a little child learning to ride a bicycle. You may have fallen and hurt yourself. You may still need training wheels. That does not mean that you are less lovable than another child who has mastered bike riding. You will learn it, too, if you keep trying. And then you won't be any more precious. You will, however, be able to go places on your bike. That's it. A grown person is not more lovable than a child, just different. It's all about growing through our experiences and keeping an open mind, even during hard times.

The most important aspect of the mastery of life is to forgive yourself for who you are, for who you are not, for what you have done, and for what you haven't done. You can develop self-esteem by doing estimable acts today. Live the paradox of owning your suffering, embracing your flaws, and accepting your truth—and watch yourself recover and blossom. It is your nature to heal.

In recovery we embark on a process of reorientation, where we give ourselves permission to have a good life. A plan for a life with dignity and integrity, one that includes making amends, can help us stay clear of self-hatred. We engage in a process of liberation from damaging habits, and gradually we relinquish the need for self-defeating and self-destructive acting out.

SELF-LOVE

I N MY EARLY SOBRIETY I stayed at a sober living house where a woman told me: "Jasmin, you are allowed to be happy today." I was so surprised—and grateful, too. I had not known. So I asked her if she would tell me every day, and she did. It was sweet. It grew on me. If you are an alcoholic, you may not be a natural at giving yourself permission to be happy and self-love is probably not your forte. Nobody in their right mind destroys their body and their life like we do. We lack self-respect and self-love. This is the source of our frantic attempts to find a little happiness where we can find it.

At some point early on, you may have learned that love hurts—and have thus gone through life interpreting pain for love and the intensity of betrayal for the kind of love you cannot be without. You may have taken abuse for intimacy. You may have been hiding your wounds when you felt like crying and screaming. You may have found excitement in seeking danger and sabotaging your well-being. As a result, you may feel guilty and ashamed and secretly think that you don't deserve better or that love without pain is boring. You don't have to put up with intimidation, manipulation, deceit, betrayal, and humiliation, but if you do, you don't have to call it "love." You may have believed that you have to put up with everything in the name of love and loyalty. Even that's not necessarily true.

I am here to remind you that, in spite of everything, you are allowed to be happy today. Whether you have done "bad" things, or whether you have allowed physical and/or emotional abuse to continue. If you love someone and they love you, that does not mean that you have to be together if it hurts. You deserve to be treated with respect and kindness. You have a right for a second chance. You can make amends to others and to yourself.

If you are just getting clean and sober, you may need a little time to get to where you feel that you deserve good things, that you are perfect, whole, and complete just the way you are. You can give yourself permission to have a good life. All the beautiful things in this world? You deserve them. God has created you just the way you are so that you may have some room to grow. You have been given strength so that you can endure and overcome adversity. You are endowed with the Divine power to heal and move on. Once you understand that no one has the right to hurt you, you will set boundaries. When you know that you deserve to be loved, you will make it happen. You can find out for yourself that you won't be bored when you walk in the light.

SENSE OF SELF

ASTERY IS A CONCEPT of child development that relates to setting a goal, making an effort, and waiting for gratification at a later point in time. This accomplishment is rewarded by gradually developing one's sense of self—and a deep sense of satisfaction and joy about oneself. Alcoholics typically remain stuck in an earlier developmental stage of immediate need gratification. Unwilling to endure the tension of delayed physical pleasure, we sacrifice meaningful goals—thereby robbing ourselves continually of this source of power and self-esteem.

Then we remain in constant need for attention, confirmation, and approval—and uncertainty, as the power is given to others to grant or withhold the desired response. The resulting persistent anxiety and low self-esteem sets in motion and reinforces a vicious cycle of aimlessness, a general lack of success experiences and satisfaction, and, subsequently, an ongoing need for control as well as sensual and artificial means of comfort. These needs are then experienced as insatiable because a human being requires more than sex, thrills, and chemicals to achieve a sense of fulfillment and wholeness—and life becomes futile. An alcoholic life is a life of being at the mercy of one's relentless neediness, as chemicals and the actions of others can never provide what a human being requires for satisfaction.

In recovery we learn to take our spirit back from these excessive attachments to things outside of ourselves. We are taught to "dress up and show up," to make ourselves useful, and to let go of the insistence on getting things from the outside. This relieves our self-obsessed fear of not being good enough, replaces it with a sense of being grounded in the present moment, and enables us to utilize the full power of our spirit. The process of mastery allows us to claim our abilities and special talents to create something worthwhile, and we develop our sense of self, find self-esteem, and discover the joy of life—even when no one is watching.

TO HELL & BACK

NOT YOUR RECIPES FOR MY HAPPINESS

Don't tell me about your success, nor your recipes for my happiness.

—Lyrics from "Rich Folks Hoax" by Rodriguez

IN ADOLESCENCE we are meant to outgrow parental dominance and become our own person. It is a transitory stage where we identify with our peers. Some people get stuck in that phase— eternally defiant, making their whole life about resistance. In the famous James Dean movie *Rebel Without a Cause,* a group of adolescents are all about looking cool and seeking thrills. Although their opposition to the depressing world of their elders didn't provide a way out, the youth culture was born.

Throughout the ages, we have murdered our spiritual masters—and our elders are busy trying to look young. These days the media presents us with an overwhelming global predicament, untrustworthy political leaders, and immature and troubled role models. No consolation or guidance to be had. Since the propagated ideals (such as staying thin and wearing label clothes) do not offer tools for living, many people become confused and depressed. With their attention permanently focused on the resistance against becoming a mature adult, they don't get anywhere. A generalized defiance does not contain the potential for success of any kind. Fear and anger distract us from freely exploring our wishes and dreams—and chemical sedation then becomes tempting. The pursuit of power and dominance over others doesn't do the trick, either. The more confused and insecure we feel inside, the more we like to control "people, places, and things." Too bad it doesn't work out that way. By being over-controlling or defiant, we disregard who we are—and fail to nurture the ground for our own prosperity.

The alternative then would be to find one's goal, wish, dream, something to go toward, something to live for. The joy of life lies in creating one's life, not in resisting others. Power is gained by living one's truth. As a result of being on the spiritual path, we look at what we can do at the moment—rather than what all the others are doing. We are meant to bring the light of a higher consciousness into our present environment. The evolution of our consciousness, which carries with it the potential for finding meaning and purpose, is an inside job. We may not be "happy, joyous, and free" all the time, but we can live in acceptance of what is. It's all about welcoming the world, doing the right thing, and sharing what makes you smile.

RHYTHM

Before enlightenment chop wood and carry water.
After enlightenment chop wood and carry water.

—Zen proverb

VERYTHING FOLLOWS ITS INTERNAL RHYTHM. The particles within the atom do, the planets do, and the biological processes in our bodies do, too. We enjoy the rhythm of music because it reinforces the internal rhythm of our heartbeat. When we feel calm and relaxed, our breath is even. Health requires regularity and stability. When we live according to a daily rhythm, where we eat, drink, and sleep according to a regular schedule, we tend to feel comfortable.

When we live a roller-coaster kind of lifestyle, we exhaust ourselves and make ourselves sick. A heart that keeps skipping beats spells danger. Continuous excitement, deprivation, and danger wear us out. Why then do addicts live chaotic lives without any order or stability? It is because we have made the pursuit of some substance our primary purpose above all else, running for something that by its very nature cannot deliver enough. We have been living a frantic life of yearning and drama without the nurture and peace we need. The result of not following our natural internal rhythm is, of course, disorder, unstable mental and physical health, and chaos all around.

In sobriety we stop running from ourselves. We learn to replace the breathless pursuit of something outside of ourselves with the quiet, calm awareness of our internal rhythm. We begin to establish a regular schedule to introduce the stability of a daily rhythm into our life. As we keep the focus on recovery, we get our life in order, too.

A PACT WITH THE DEVIL

HE AGE-OLD GERMAN LEGEND *Doctor Faustus* describes how a man, frustrated with human limitations and lack of happiness, falls prey to the seductive offerings of Mephistopheles (AKA the devil). Faustus's desires lead him astray, and he makes a pact with Mephistopheles to serve Faustus until he would experience a moment of bliss, at which time Mephistopheles could take Faustus's life and his soul. The pursuit of lust and euphoria at any cost progresses into tragedy for Faustus and Gretchen, the woman who loves him.

What alcoholic couldn't relate to this character? Aren't we just like him? Having experienced life's adversity, we have succumbed to the temptations of endless pleasure and oblivion. We forgot about the purpose of our life and we achieved amnesia from our soul's mission. When we neglected our soul, our life became meaningless. In our despair, we were left with the exclusive and elusive pursuit of physical satisfaction. It was as though our addiction turned into the hellish attempt to quench our thirst with salt water and we became progressively crazed with thirst.

We must understand in our innermost being that it cannot work, ever. We have pursued an error. While we starve our soul, a murderous thirst arises within, resulting in lust, greed, gluttony, sloth, anger, pride, and envy, where we rip from life and from other people what we think we must have to satisfy our needs. "A pact with the devil" is a metaphor for refusing the gift of human consciousness and instead giving in to that part within that tempts us to retreat from everything for a moment of relief, which we call pleasure.

We are torn by ambivalence and conflict between what we want and…what we want. As soon as we decide to go with recovery, we also want to avoid discomfort; we look for relief from our inner struggle, and we want it instantly. We desire the benefits of a new life, but are ever ready to go back to the life we know. We are stuck between incompatibles, so we don't like to commit to anything.

Without meaning, our life is sad and empty and exhausting for no good reason. We have thought that we must get high, when we really sought happiness and peace that comes from being on the right path. Even though it may feel that way, the agitation inside is not the enemy. Rather, it is the voice of intuition crying for recognition. The solution is not to silence it, but to hear it. Only then can we find the right path.

Recovery from addiction, then, means recovering the conscious awareness of our soul's mission on earth. As a result, we become willing to endure what it takes to pick up the pieces of the destruction we have caused while being oblivious. Little by little we become unstuck, grow up, find our purpose, and weave our spirit into a life worth living. Becoming conscious is a process. It may take a minute or two. Have some faith and a little patience while you are transcending into the light.

TWO WOLVES ARE FIGHTING IN MY HEART

"I feel like I have two wolves fighting in my heart,"
the grandfather tells his grandson.
"One wolf is vengeful, angry, and violent.
The other wolf is loving and compassionate."
"Which wolf will win the fight in your heart, Grandpa?"
his little grandson asks.
"The one I feed," he explains.

—Native American Story

INNER CONFLICT, or ambivalence, has been described as "two souls dwelling in my chest" or "two wolves fighting in my heart." Freud referred to the opposing forces within as "Eros and Thanatos"—the forces of love/sex versus death/destructiveness, respectively. Some alcoholics are kind and decent while sober, but when under the influence another side comes out— angry and scary—as depicted in the famous movie *Doctor Jekyll and Mister Hyde*. They end up lonely when their friends shy away from their unpredictable "crazy" behavior, while preferring the comfort of being in trustworthy company, where they don't have to walk on eggshells.

Most alcoholics are torn between the desire for continued well-being and the compulsion to self-destruct. Without resolving our conflicts, we keep catering to the destructive forces in spite of good intentions and resolutions not to do so, and we remain desperate and hopeless. Inner struggles can be excruciating in their intensity, using up an enormous amount of our energy and leaving us depleted and incapable of dealing with external issues. As a consequence, we experience low self-esteem, self-loathing, and shame, which furthers our self-defeating behaviors. That part within that needs a positive sense of self is being starved, so it weakens. The less power we assert for integration of all aspects of our personality, the more we experience impulsive self-destructive tendencies as a threatening foreign force within, which causes anxiety as our self-confidence, hope, and courage wither away.

We use denial and repression to defend against the truth about ourselves. Our disowned parts become our demons—strange, powerful, and scary entities. And, as you know, our demons are not silenced by lying to ourselves. Delusion has brought them into existence in the first place. Resistance keeps them around. As you seek the absence of fear, your focus is on fear and so you feed it. The solution lies in being humble and accepting who you are, flaws and all. Your lies can never be as powerful as your truth. You don't have to be afraid anymore that your flaws define you. It's part of who you are. It's part of being human like the rest of us. Keep the focus on faith and courage. Even if you feel a little like David who had to fight Goliath, you will learn how to manage your disease. He did win against all odds.

DEMONS & DESIRES

IMAGINE HAVING RECEIVED A BALLOON FOR EVERY DAY OF YOUR LIFE

TO BLOW YOUR LIFE INTO, SO YOU WOULD REMEMBER.

THINGS HAPPENED, YOU GOT SCARED,

YOU BLEW YOUR FEAR INTO YOUR BALLOONS,

AND YOU PAINTED SCARY FACES ON THEM TO REMEMBER IT ALL.

YOU FORGOT IT ALL,

YOU TOOK YOUR BALLOONS FOR DEMONS,

AND YOU BECAME AFRAID OF YOUR OWN BALLOONS.

YOU THOUGHT YOU HAD TO RUN AWAY FROM THEM.

THEN YOU WANTED WHAT YOU DIDN'T HAVE,

SO YOU BLEW YOUR DESIRES INTO SOME BALLOONS,

AND YOU HELD ON TO THEM, TIGHTLY, AND RAN WITH THEM.

MEANWHILE, YOU LOST YOUR WAY.

YOU CAN STOP NOW.

CATCH YOUR BREATH AND TAKE A LOOK AROUND, AFTER ALL THIS TIME.

YOU WILL SEE THAT YOU CAN LET GO ANYTIME YOU LIKE,

AND OPEN YOUR HANDS TO RECEIVE THE PRESENT.

FROM NOW ON, YOU CAN PAINT SMILEY FACES (OR SOMETHING DIFFERENT)

ON YOUR BALLOONS INSTEAD.

ALCOHOLISM IS NOT ABOUT ALCOHOL—IT'S ABOUT TRYING TO FORGET.

AND RECOVERY IS NOT ABOUT NOT DRINKING—IT'S ABOUT SEEKING THE TRUTH,

HAVING SOME FAITH, AND REGAINING YOUR LIFE.

THE GOLDEN KEY

On coming home at night, Mr. A finds his neighbor Mr. B searching for something on the ground underneath the streetlight. Mr. A asks Mr. B what he is looking for and Mr. B tells him that he is looking for his lost key. So Mr. A proceeds to help him look for the key. When, after looking for some time, they are not able to locate the key, Mr. A finally asks: "Are you sure you lost your key right here, under this light?" Mr. B answers: "No, but it's too dark over there, where I lost it, to find anything."

—Author Unknown

WHEN YOU WERE SEEKING HAPPINESS, you looked for alcohol/drugs. When you needed love, you found "casual" sex. This caused unbearable suffering—your spirit became attached to things outside of yourself, where you have no power. You have been looking for happiness and love in the wrong places. No matter how long you look, you won't find it—because it is not there.

In early sobriety, you might be tempted to go back to the sources of quick oblivion to find relief from your feelings. That's what we do—when we feel lost, we fall back on our experiences and memories. However, just like Mr. B, you will not find your key where it isn't. If you haven't found it yet—don't give up. The golden key is where it has been all along. Even though it has been hidden underneath your fear and confusion, you can and will find it—if you keep looking in the right place: within yourself. Pull your spirit back from attachments outside of yourself. Your experience has taught you that you have been looking in the wrong place. Make it through the day sober, one day at a time, and the dark gray fog of doom and gloom will dissipate—and you will find your golden key.

In recovery we are meant to learn endurance; we must sustain our newly found hope, and make our sobriety our number one priority—even though it requires sitting with our feelings without acting out. Focus on your breath, notice exactly where these feelings are located in your body, and allow them to be what they are. Although you may feel uncomfortable, you will notice that the feelings are not unbearable. You have been living with them for so long; it will not get any worse than what you already know. I admit that early sobriety can be difficult at times, just as with any recovery from a long and severe illness. Keep in mind that you are in the process of healing. You will get well, even without any effort. Recovery from addiction happens by itself—you WILL recover, as long as you give your body and mind a chance to heal.

> *Happiness is a by-product of living the right kind of a life,*
> *of doing the right thing. Do not search for happiness,*
> *search for right living and happiness will be your reward.*
>
> —Richmond Walker, *Twenty-Four Hours a Day*

THE MAGIC OF THE SPOKEN WORD

WHILE WE LIVE IN OUR DISEASE, we dwell in dis-ease—compelled by the frantic urge to recreate some semblance of comfort. This remains our prime priority. Our interactions are subject to this need and we express our misery to others, oblivious to the effect we have on them. Stuck in a downward spiral of self-destruction, we tear them down with us. Without self-respect, we don't speak in a respectful manner. As we experience ourselves as helpless and powerless victims, we like to look for fault elsewhere, and so we judge, criticize, and blame others for everything that goes wrong. We make it hard for everyone to deal with us. We ruin their mood when we make promises we don't keep and lie whenever we want to escape the consequences. Our verbalizations become recklessly aggressive or whiney, while we refuse to acknowledge the obvious. In the process, we deprive ourselves of accurate understanding and create confusion in our own minds. Meanwhile, we fail to formulate meaningful life goals or to present ourselves to the world in a favorable light, and our life becomes progressively difficult.

In recovery we get to examine how we are expressing our thoughts and to adjust some of our habitual behaviors. This is our opportunity to seize the power of the spoken word, stop deceitful and hurtful verbalizations, and become aware of the life we bring into existence as we speak. The twelve steps of Alcoholics Anonymous are a formula for identifying destructive thought patterns and replacing them with the truth. We are shown how to take our power back from resentments, and we begin to present ourselves with humility and dignity. We can pick up recovery tools for decent conduct, where we respect other people's boundaries. We refrain from imposing our will on others. Instead, we listen and try to understand them. We use the spoken word in prayer and kind verbal interactions, where we are mindful never to hurt anyone. As a result, the toxic dwelling place we came to inhabit turns into a friendly and prosperous environment for our dreams to manifest.

THE GARDEN OF LIFE

WHEN WE ARE BORN, we are ready to take our place. We look around with interest and curiosity to see what it's like over here. They give us some seeds, tools, potions, and poisons, and they proceed to teach us good, bad, useful, and useless things. We have some time to learn how to make it all work out. Then we are faced with tasks so that we may grow and develop through our challenges. It's a trial-and-error kind of thing. Circumstances change, and we must stay flexible and lively. Occasionally it's necessary to adapt and adjust our ways. Some of us get overwhelmed and intimidated by it all—and begin to invest in resistance. If that happens, we can get stuck in generalized defiance, and things don't work out all that well.

Imagine your place like a garden, with unique characteristics and circumstances depending on your lot in life. Some of us are presented with a friendly and mild environment, while others are meant to survive a rough climate, struggle with harsh conditions, and thrive on stony ground. It is what it is. Know that your place requires consistent attendance for planting, fertilizing, and watering—it's on you to create the garden you like. Without your loving care, your life garden will deteriorate, even if you were endowed with the best potential. Some things will come easily and naturally; others cannot get established in spite of all your efforts. If you find yourself at the Bering Sea in Alaska, don't try to grow palm trees. Look into fishing…

Some people create the space they would like to inhabit—magnificent gardens with shade-giving fruit trees and colorful flowers. Others don't feel like looking after their own place and fantasize about faraway gardens, which would be better. They end up feeling dysfunctional, defeated, envious, and angry—more or less aware that they are not doing what they ought to be. In order to forget about their disappointment in themselves, they close their eyes to reality. After a while they feel ashamed, lose confidence, and act as though they don't care. From time to time, they may get some flowers from their neighbor's garden—and cry when these flowers wilt.

All that is alive grows—the good and the bad. Some weeds grow even more quickly than the plants you desire. If your garden has been neglected for a long time, it could have deteriorated into a wasteland by now, and you might not like to be in your place. Examine what's going on, and you will figure out what you can do about it. If you don't want the weeds to take over, you must remove them and make room for new sprigs and sprouts. All you need is the willingness to show up for today's work, with humility to learn how to do it right. Be reasonable with your expectations. Remember that things take their own time to mature. As long as you are active, productive, and creative, you will grow, prosper, and blossom along with all that you bring into life. Self-confidence comes as you master today's tasks, one at a time. Make yourself useful. The joy of life is found by nurturing life.

WILLINGNESS

YOU CAN BE LOVING AND OPEN—OR FEARFUL AND DEFENSIVE.

YOU CAN STAY IN DEFIANCE—OR DECIDE TO LET IT BE WHAT IT IS.

YOU CAN WELCOME THE WORLD AND PROGRESS—

OR WITHDRAW FROM IT AND REGRESS.

YOU CAN PROCEED THROUGH THE TUNNELS ON YOUR PATH

AND COME OUT ON THE OTHER SIDE—

OR GIVE UP AND TURN AROUND IN DARKNESS.

YOU CAN BE RESISTANT TO THE UNIVERSE—OR ALIGNED WITH THE DIVINE FORCES.

YOU CAN FIGHT AGAINST WHAT OTHERS WANT—OR CREATE WHAT YOU WANT.

YOU CAN FOCUS ON BEING LOVING AND USEFUL—

OR ACT ON NEED, GREED, AND GLUTTONY.

YOU CAN GIVE AND SHARE—

OR TRY TO TAKE ADVANTAGE OF OTHERS AND TAKE WHAT THEY HAVE.

YOU CAN GET LOADED ALL NIGHT LONG—OR SHOW UP FOR YOUR DAY.

YOU CAN USE YOUR GIFTS TO BE OF SERVICE—OR YOU CAN BE USELESS.

YOU CAN MAKE A COMMITMENT TO REALITY—OR RETREAT INTO A FAKE WORLD OF

DENIAL, DECEIT, MANIPULATION, AND CONFUSION.

YOU CAN BECOME ALL THAT YOU CAN BE IN THIS LIFE—

OR SEEK TO AVOID ANYTHING UNPLEASANT.

YOU CAN STAY IN SELF-OBSESSED FEAR—OR IN HUMBLE ACCEPTANCE.

YOU CAN ISOLATE YOURSELF—OR BRING LOVE WHEREVER YOU GO.

YOU CAN BE RESENTFUL AND MISERABLE—OR COMPASSIONATE AND KIND.

YOU CAN USE YOUR TIME TO MASTER YOUR TASKS ONE BY ONE—

OR WASTE YOUR TIME WITH THE FUTILE FIGHT AGAINST WINDMILLS.

YOU CAN MATURE AND AGE GRACEFULLY—OR FAIL AT RESISTING NATURE.

YOU CAN DEVOTE YOUR TIME TO BLOSSOMING—OR STAY BARREN.

YOU CAN HAVE A LIFE—OR LOOK ON WITH SADNESS, RESENTMENT,

AND ENVY TO OTHERS WHO DO.

YOU CAN COMMIT YOURSELF TO GROWING AND OVERCOMING OBSTACLES—

OR FEEL DEFECTIVE.

YOU CAN DO WHAT IT TAKES TO HAVE SUCCESS—OR FEEL LIKE A LOSER.

YOU CAN STAND UP FOR YOURSELF—OR BE AT THE MERCY OF OTHERS.

YOU CAN CONTINUE TO "LIVE" IN THE PAST—

OR RECOVER FROM A SEEMINGLY HOPELESS STATE OF MIND.

YOU CAN DECIDE TO RECOVER AND BECOME WHOLE—

OR STUBBORNLY INSIST ON KEEPING YOUR PAST PAIN ALIVE

AND STAY WOUNDED AND FRAGMENTED.

YOU CAN PROJECT YOUR WOUND ONTO OTHERS AND BLAME THEM—

OR ATTEND TO IT AND HEAL.

YOU CAN TUNE IN TO HARMONY AND BALANCE—

OR DEFIANTLY BRING ABOUT DISCORD.

YOU CAN LIVE IN THE LIGHT—OR DWELL IN DARKNESS.

YOU CAN USE DRUGS—OR CHOOSE RECOVERY.

IT'S UP TO YOU.

INITIATION

IF ADDICTION MEANS a pact with the devil, where one sacrifices everything for a moment of bliss, recovery signifies the triumph of the human spirit over the powers of destruction—against all odds. Initiation refers to mastering the required, most difficult, and dangerous task in order to belong to a tribe. It is implied that one must prove one's courage and outstanding physical and mental strength to qualify for admission. This explains why recovering alcoholics wear their AA membership like a badge of honor—and with a smile. They have overcome a seemingly hopeless state of mind—and turned their fate around. The alcoholic's total letting go of the life that they know in order to arrive at the "promised land" of some unknown spirituality qualifies as initiatory rite of passage.

They say: "As long as you think like you always did, you will do what you always did, and get what you got." When you "hit bottom," it is evident that you can go no further. As horrible as it is, it appears to be necessary to "die" to your old life so that you abandon your stubborn and tenacious hold on your old ideas. To have a good life, you must be able to utilize your brain in the best way possible. As a result of rescuing your brain from drowning in a toxic chemical soup, you move from surviving to transcending to thriving. Reclaiming the clarity of your mental capacity signifies a rebirth to a new life where you can be open, humble, and teachable, just like a little child looking for guidance.

Faith in the guidance of a benevolent Higher Power supports the plunge into the unknown. You are given a second chance in this life to set things right, to undo your errors and mistakes and find forgiveness. The initiatory task requires a cleansing renewal of your attitude, where you examine your actions and courageously endure what must be experienced. As you find redemption from your wrongs, you begin to feel free from your burden.

The description of our new life can be summarized as follows: "Clean house, trust God, help others." This is hardly a desirable recipe for a hedonistic alcoholic, and yet, as the result of our transformation, it spells the delicious sweetness of serenity and peace.

TIME IS ON MY SIDE

I am drinking to forget that I am drinking.

—Dr. Erika Mueller (book title translated from German)

THE BOOK TITLE QUOTED ABOVE depicts the co-existence of con-
flicting desires, which is typical for alcoholics. Reluctant to
surrender to an unknown new life, addicts may try to go north
and south at the same time, and end up stuck in perennial conflict, repeating the difficult phase of early recovery, when the
alcoholic mind is struggling to accept reality and establish a
solid sense of self. Some of us wish to get sober, but also hold
on to the desire to take the edge off or "party" with old friends,
while denying that dire consequences would arise again, just
like they did before. The fun times of inebriation in the old days
are remembered in "euphoric recall," and so they may relapse
after having gone through the agony of withdrawal again and
again—in spite of their hopes and best intentions. After having listened closely to their experience, thoughts, and feelings,
I have found that some things stand out.

While we are using, our world is focused on getting high
and procuring the means to avoid withdrawal. This takes up all
our energy. We lose interest in other activities. In early recovery,

we find that we "don't have a life"—nothing to do and nobody who truly seeks our presence. We want to feel good now and always, but we haven't been building up relationships, activities, and skills that are enjoyable. We are left with empty time all day long where we think about our problems and feel uncomfortable. We don't like that. Patience is not our strongest feature. Eventually some of us relapse because we lose confidence that all of that will ever change.

What is different about those people who stay sober? It is their surrender to "a new life," much in the same way they had previously surrendered to the using life—at any cost. Everything in life has a price—as long as you are willing to pay the price for getting loaded, you will do that. Getting sober also has a price—you must be humble enough to learn a new life, a new language, a new way of thinking, and different behaviors, much like a child does. If you are arrogant and think that you are too old or too smart for learning this, you will give up.

It is strenuous, just like starting to learn a foreign language or a new sport. All new abilities require some effort and perseverance. The fun comes as you see some progress. You gain confidence as you think, "I can do this." Recovery is the process of learning how to have a fulfilling life—with integrity and successful activities and relationships. You build self-esteem as you do estimable acts. You find purpose in life as you do meaningful things. But don't believe what I say. Check it out for yourself! Give it a chance! When you have outgrown drugs, you can move on from them, even in spite of sweet memories—just like an old lover who made you happy once upon a time. It's just not working anymore. Time to go. Let's see what else there is.

RELAPSE

ECAUSE WE'RE APPLYING all of our mental capacities toward using, we don't have a life left that's worth living. Our people have been looking at us with anger and contempt for too long. Their hearts have been broken. We are broken, too. Until we have burnt our bridges and thoroughly destroyed all that is precious in our life, we don't really consider getting clean and sober. In early recovery, we are overwhelmed with shame and self-loathing as we look at the trail of broken dreams and broken promises we have left behind. So we go through the agony of detoxing as if the world depended on it—and for us, it does. We try to believe that there is hope, that we can be healed. We concentrate on making it through the day—and with help, we do. We get some faith and a little confidence back. We connect with a Higher Power; we begin to feel alive again, renewed, and grateful. And then, just when it would get a little less horrible, many of us relapse. It's a baffling phenomenon—heartbreaking to watch, and devastating for anybody who cares about us. What is going on that makes us destroy the tender little flower of hope that has been nurtured for a moment?

In our disease, we experience being with ourselves and others as so severely unpleasant that we seek to change or erase our awareness—at any cost. I have asked many addicts what their thoughts and feelings were at the time of relapse. I have never heard any convincing pro-relapse arguments and nobody ever told me that they were happy about it. There seems to be a vague sense of boredom or loneliness, some hopelessness about their longing for safety, love, or sex that sets in motion an indifference about their future—a barely noticeable shift in focus from interest in life to negation of self for the mere chance at a moment of bliss, or at least oblivion. At that instant, they get back to the death-defying willingness to give their soul in trade for a minute of "time out" from reality. The surrender to a Higher Power is reversed to the illusion of self-control. Humility and truth are replaced with ego and deceit. Instead of faith and hope, the result is fear and blame. Impatience takes us from the slow path of recovery back to the dire straits of hopeless but familiar misery.

Alcoholism is a chronic and progressive disease requiring patience for neurological and psychic change. The reconstruction of our life and of ourselves challenges our endurance. Sorry, but the party is over and there is no quick fix. Addicts can get lost in a masochistic and exhausting relapse loop. They seek relief and find hell, again and again and again. The way out cannot be found by turning back. It can only be reached by walking through—towards the light.

MIRAGE

SOME DESERT TRAVELERS SEE A MIRAGE

AND FALL PREY TO THE VISION OF A PLACE

WHERE THEY WOULD FIND THE DELICIOUS WATER OF RESCUE.

THEY NEVER GET THERE. THEY DIE OF THIRST.

ADDICTION IS SUCH A TRAGIC MISTAKE.

IN OUR EXPERIENCE OF FEELING LOST,

WE FIND OURSELVES LIKE A THIRSTY TRAVELER IN THE DESERT.

WITHOUT A CONSCIOUS CONTACT TO A HIGHER POWER,

WE ARE TEMPTED TO FALL FOR ILLUSIONS.

IN PURSUIT OF THE PROMISED RELIEF,

AN ADDICT GETS LOST IN A CHEMICALLY CREATED VIRTUAL REALITY

AND LOSES THE WORLD.

EVENTUALLY HE ABANDONS ALL INTEREST IN REALITY

AND INSISTS ON MAINTAINING HIS DELUSIONS AT ALL COST.

MEANWHILE, HE GIVES UP THE SEARCH FOR THE RIGHT PATH,

BECOMES DELIRIOUS, AND PERISHES.

To get out of the desert, it is essential to remember
that life cannot be sustained in a fictitious mental world,
even if it takes away your hopelessness for a little while.
You have been endowed with gifts and assets,
which you must utilize to find your path.

You will find happiness
as you overcome the obstacles and show up for your people.
The thirst of your soul will be quenched
when you discover and develop your talents
during the brief moment in time you have on this planet.

FINAL THOUGHTS

STILL STANDING

I WAS LEFT EXHAUSTED AND DEFEATED

FROM TRYING TO ESCAPE THE CHAOS I MANIFESTED.

EVERYTHING RAN THROUGH MY FINGERS.

WHATEVER I HAD WANTED—

IT BECAME MEANINGLESS WHEN I TOUCHED IT.

NOTHING TO HOLD AND TO UNDERSTAND.

MY YEARNING HAD CREATED MY PAIN.

THE FULFILLMENT OF MY WISHES

HAD MADE MY LIFE UNMANAGEABLE.

THAT'S HOW CREATIVE I AM.

THAT'S HOW POWERFUL I AM.

THAT'S HOW IGNORANT I AM.

KNOWING THAT I DID IT ALL—

I AM STILL HERE AND I AM SMILING.

THESE DAYS, IT DOESN'T HAVE TO BE WHAT IT ISN'T.

TWELVE-STEP PROGRAMS

Alcoholics Anonymous (AA)—323-936-4343, 800-923-8722
Narcotics Anonymous (NA)—562-698-4604, 800-TODAYNA
Al-Anon (for people affected by someone else's
    drinking)—818-760-7122, 888-684-6444
Alateen is part of Al-Anon (for young people under 20)
Co-Dependents Anonymous (CoDA)—323-969-4995,
    602-277-7991
Sex-and-Love Addicts Anonymous (SLA)—617-332-1845
Incest-Survivors Anonymous (ISA)—562-428-5599

This is NOT a complete list of all Twelve-Step Programs—please call AA's main office for inquiries about related programs, or look it up on the internet. If you are unsure about which program most relates to you, just attend a meeting in your area.

There is no commitment required, and attendance is free of charge.

If you have a history of relapse in spite of your best intentions, chances are you have not addressed your core addiction. Finding recovery may be more important than avoiding this issue out of shame... Remember, it's an anonymous program attended by people who have similar problems. It will be very comforting to find out that you are not alone with this.

SPIRITUAL BOOKS
TO SUPPORT YOUR RECOVERY

Alcoholics Anonymous

Big Book

Twelve Steps and Twelve Traditions

Melody Beattie

The Language of Letting Go

Codependent No More

Don Miguel Ruiz

The Four Agreements

The Mastery of Love

Deepak Chopra

The Seven Spiritual Laws of Success

The Book of Secrets

Pat Rodegast

Emmanuel's Book I, II, and III

Caroline Myss

Anatomy of the Spirit

Why People Don't Heal and How They Can

Gurmukh Kaur Khalsa

The Eight Human Talents

Thich Nhat Hanh

Teachings on Love

Patrick Carnes

Out of the Shadows

The Betrayal Bond

Charlotte Davis Kasl

Women, Sex, and Addiction

Paulo Coelho

The Alchemist

Veronika Decides to Die

Clarissa Pinkola Estes

Women Who Run with the Wolves

CREDITS

We gratefully acknowledge the copyright holders of the following works:

Peck, M. Scott, *The Road Less Traveled*. Copyright © 1978 by M. Scott Peck. New York: Simon and Schuster, 1978.

Rodriguez, "Rich Folks Hoax" lyrics. Rodriguez, 1968. Reprinted with permission.

Rogg, Jesse and Samuel Falson, "Too Many Questions" words and music by Jesse Rogg and Samuel Falson © 2008, reproduced by permission of EMI Music Publishing Ltd, Tux.E.Do LLC and Sparro LLC, London W8 5SW.

Estés, Clarissa Pinkola, *Women Who Run With the Wolves*. Copyright © 1992, 1995 by Clarissa Pinkola Estés, Ph.D. New York: Ballantine Books, 2003.

Walker, Richmond, *Twenty-Four Hours a Day*. © 1954, 1975 by Hazelden Foundation. All rights reserved.

ABOUT THE AUTHOR

JASMIN ROGG graduated from UCLA with a B.A. in Psychology, and from Loyola Marymount University with an M.A. in Counseling Psychology. She subsequently received her Marriage Family Therapist license in 1982. In addition to offering psychotherapy to recovering addicts and alcoholics in private practice in Los Angeles, California, she specializes in treating emotional disorders such as depression and anxiety, and has been facilitating ongoing recovery groups in various chemical dependency treatment centers for years.

Having spent many years in the field of addiction and recovery, on both a professional and personal level, she knows what it takes to leave behind destructive behavior patterns in favor of actions that promote prosperity and success, and has dedicated her life to using her extensive experience to benefit others. In her work she utilizes the "alchemy" of turning weakness into strength, passing on resources and tools for recovery from emotional pain, depression, anxiety, and addiction—for building a good life.

In the seventies Jasmin moved to Los Angeles from her native Germany in order to broaden her horizons. Her family background is Jewish-Romanian-Italian. She is bilingual in English and German, and also speaks some Romanian and French.

After various migrations and detours she lives in Los Angeles, next door to her married son in a big household with her extended chosen family, guests from all over the world, as well as cats and dogs (and cautiously visiting birds, squirrels, opossums, skunks, and raccoons).

www.JasminRogg.com